WITHDRAWN

Major Themes
in
Prize-Winning American Drama

by

JANE F. BONIN

with a Preface by

Paul T. Nolan

The Scarecrow Press, Inc.
Metuchen, N. J.   1975

Library of Congress Cataloging in Publication Data

Bonin, Jane F
  Major themes in prize-winning American drama.

  Bibliography: p.
  Includes index.
  1. American drama--20th century--History and criti-
cism. 2. Literary prizes. I. Title.
PS351.B59   812'.5'409   74-34492
ISBN 0-8108-0799-8

For Paul T. Nolan
teacher, colleague, friend

TABLE OF CONTENTS

DISCOVERING AMERICA'S DRAMATIC LITERATURE

For the past seven years I have been aware of two books being written by Dr. Jane F. Bonin, this one and her earlier bibliographical and descriptive guide, <u>Prize-Winning Drama in America</u> (Scarecrow, 1973). In the making of these two books, I have played approximately the same role that the Best Man plays to the Groom. I have listened, agreed, and--when I did not agree--I knew that it was the better part of valor to hold my tongue.

Now that Scarecrow has asked me to write a few comments upon this work, however, I am free to confess the reasons that I have agreed to be the Best Man, a duty that is not easy to accept casually when the Groom is sincere and the match is a love affair. What Dr. Bonin has done in this book, <u>Major Themes in America's Prize-Winning Drama</u>, and in her earlier study is to establish a geography for American drama.

As an historical fact, of course, American drama has been around for the past two and a half centuries, ever since 1714 when Governor Robert Hunter vented his spleen against his fellow New Yorkers by satirizing them in a much undervalued farce, <u>Androborus</u>. But as late as 1920, it was still fashionable among "serious" American drama critics to wonder if there was such a thing as "American" drama, or whether it was not merely an unfortunate imitation of European drama.

Dr. Bonin's first book made a simple approach to that problem. If America had produced a body of plays that were both American and of sufficient quality to be called "dramatic literature," such works should have some sort of community status. She turned to those plays that had won awards, those plays that, in the opinion of people seriously concerned with the drama, showed superior merit.

Dr. Bonin has called attention, of course, to the fact that some of these plays are less than masterpieces. She has also called attention to the fact that some plays not included have, in the opinion of serious critics, been more deserving of awards. Both of these conditions are, to be sure, limitations that should be considered in evaluating American drama. The prize-winning American drama, it seems safe to say, is better than "representative." At the same time, however, it is not "all" of the best drama that exists. Dr. Bonin laments that no play by Clifford Odets is included. I lament the fact that George Kaufmann and Marc Connelly's Merton of the Movies is not included. Any drama critic dealing with American drama, however, would rather be limited to these prize-winning plays than attempt to make a list of "best" plays that excluded them. If these plays were all that we had of American drama, we would be as well served as we are with the forty-some plays that now represent all of Greek drama.

Dr. Bonin's first book, Prize-Winning Drama, is, to be sure, much simpler to justify as a "geography" of American drama. Her present study probably needs some explanation on several fronts. This preface, of course, has no intention of anticipating the defense made in the final chapter. It does seem to me, however, that emphasis needs to be placed upon what this book does not do as well as what it does.

viii

The critic looking for a formal explication of a single play needs to look elsewhere, to Modern Drama or the American Quarterly, for example. One might, in fact, criticize the title Major Themes in.... The title, Major Assumptions in American Drama, might be closer to the mark. What this book does is to analyze some eighty plays not in terms of what each play says as a single formal statement, but rather what all of the plays seem to assume about major themes in American life during the fifty-some years during which these plays were written.

The five themes with which Dr. Bonin worked--women and marriage, work and material rewards, war and physical violence, politics, and religion--were selected (I know from many conversations with the author) after a great deal of thought. At various times during the making of this book, Dr. Bonin had other subjects under serious consideration. One subject that seemed to require study, for example, was ethnic groups. She finally decided that the attitude toward ethnic groups was not a subject in itself, but that rather the attitude toward any ethnic groups was the result of an assumption concerning the individual, an assumption that she thought could be best understood by an analysis of the attitude toward women, individuals, and the institution, marriage, that has largely taken its shape in modern life from that attitude toward the individual. Her study of the attitude toward work and material rewards is, it seems to me, essentially a continuation of her first chapter. As the first chapter describes the role attributed to women, the second chapter essentially describes the role assigned to men in America.

The value of this book to historians and sociologists is clear enough. It should, however, also be of considerable value to anyone interested in American drama, either critically or creatively. It is a truism that drama, unlike the other literary art forms, cannot "educate" its audience easily. The novelist, for example, can always explain to his reader what he is doing; the playwright, however, knows that the play must be immediately clear. It must conform to "the idea of the theatre," as Francis Fergusson has noted, that the audience already holds. Plays are built upon other plays, not because the playwright has less imagination, but rather because he has an audience trained to look at the stage with certain assumptions.

It is true, of course, that the major assumptions--those dealing with what subjects are fit for drama, what kind of a stage is "theatrical," what is a "proper" acting style--have little to do with the subject matter of separate plays. Euripides' Trojan Women and Arthur Miller's All My Sons may say, in the main, the same thing about war and the crimes associated with it. An audience familiar with plays that use only one of these forms--the Greek tragedy or the modern problem play--would undoubtedly be offended by the play with which they were not familiar, or at least so puzzled by the form that it would cause problems in appreciation.

Although it is less true, it is also important that a critic must be aware of the thematic assumptions of a particular drama. Within the framework of these assumptions, what early American playwright, for example, could write a Why Marry? without a happy-marriage ending? If the American assumption is, as Dr. Bonin argues, that women cannot achieve happiness without marriage, the playwright who would criticize the "evils" in marriage must do so within the biases of that assumption. The critic who expects the playwright to "editorialize" against marriage in the form of the drama simply fails to understand that drama can consider assumptions, but it cannot establish new assumptions. The play can, of course, challenge any assumption, but a critic should not complain that the play is based on the very assumption that is being challenged. Some critics, with strong ideational biases, have, I recognize, complained that the "theatre has lost its mind" because of this fact; such a complaint, it seems to me, is rather like complaining that a tax audit fails to reveal the charm of the taxpayer.

Dr. Bonin's analysis of major American themes, as they are treated in the drama, gives, it seems to me, the ground rules for critical debate. Insofar as her conclusions are valid, she has established the assumptions that an American playwright had to make before he could begin his play.

As an occasional playwright, I have found her conclusions of considerable value. Her analysis of my play, The Loneliest Game, told me little about the play critically that I did not already know. It did, however, tell me a great deal about the assumptions that I made before I ever had a single thought about the play itself. My general assumption, I can see by hindsight after reading her first chapter, was that the unmarried state was certain to produce unhappiness. Only one of my seven "lonely" characters has ever been married, and that one unhappily. Again, my assumption that violence is the American way to show character--her argument in her third chapter--obviously is one that I absorbed unconsciously from my reading of American drama. I am quite certain, again by hindsight, that if I had been conscious of these assumptions, I would have made some different choices that would have, I would like to think, resulted in a better play.

The most recent American plays--those being produced in the Off-Off-Broadway theater--have, it seems to me, demonstrated a movement by American playwrights to a more conscious awareness of the assumptions made in American drama. Joel Oppenheimer's The Great American Desert, for example, draws heavily on the "frontier" drama of the late nineteenth and early twentieth-century American drama, but Mr. Oppenheimer does it consciously. Dr. Bonin's study should make it easier for all playwrights to examine their assumptions, the basic biases that they absorb with their study of their native drama.

One other group of people concerned with American literature could also profit from the reading of Dr. Bonin's two books--the makers of American literature anthologies. There is, these two books demonstrate, a larger American drama, a more important American drama, than can be represented by selecting a play by Eugene O'Neill or Edward Albee as the "only" drama that America has produced.

I have, I realize, spoken my piece in the role of Best Man, perhaps too much so. The Groom is not without faults. Dr. Bonin's two studies will, I am sure, be faulted for this or that omission, this or that commission; and the criticism will have validity. These two books, however, are a pioneer attempt to give American dramatic literature a base, a simple geography, a subject matter that has, in the main, not existed. American drama, to be sure, is part of the whole modern drama scene. A playwright, like Eugene O'Neill, for example--as Robert Brustein demonstrated in his The Theatre of Revolt--is perhaps first of all a worldwide playwright. But American drama, also, has a nature of its own, and it is impossible to evaluate the worth of any single American play without taking into account its American nature, or to assume that an American nature does not exist.

Paul T. Nolan

Lafayette, Louisiana

xii

INTRODUCTION

This study concerns itself with those American plays
which have won major drama awards since 1917, the year the
first Pulitzer Prize for Drama was awarded. This list of
winners contains some fine plays. Many, in fact, have been
judged among the best in American dramatic literature by the
severest critical standards. Others, however, have less
aesthetic interest, and a few richly deserve the obscurity into which they have sunk. Who cares, one might legitimately
ask, about Alison's House, Hell-Bent for Heaven, or Icebound? To further complicate matters, the list of these plays
conspicuously omits some plays which the prize-givers, endowed with hindsight, would surely want now to include.
Where is Awake and Sing? What happened to The Little
Foxes?

This study does not, however, consider either the critical acumen of the judges or the artistic merits and demerits
of the plays. For the purposes of this study--which is to explore America's most popular body of culturally acceptable
plays for attitudes they contain--the list is a natural one, and
the weak plays are just as revealing as the good ones. The
second-rate art of a society is so useful in understanding a
civilization that it ought not be left aside while one contem-
plates only its glories.

The underlying assumption here is that popular American drama--especially when one considers only that drama

that receives the attention of educated and critical judges--
is a sensitive barometer, not only to the public taste but to
its general concerns and attitudes as well. No playwright
can survive for long if his plays ignore or run counter to
the basic assumptions and values of the most influential critics in the community of playgoers he must serve. A collec-
tion of plays generally conceded to be the "best" in America
can, therefore, provide a useful index to the American value
system. If one wants to know what mainstream, educated
Americans have thought about love and war, about work and
play, about politics and religion--in short, about life and
death--the eighty-odd plays considered here should give some
valuable clues. Furthermore, because values and attitudes
change, one should also be able to trace through these plays,
beginning with World War I and continuing to the present,
certain shifts and moderations in moral and ethical postures.

It could be argued that playgoing New Yorkers are a
highly select group, especially when one deals with the official judges for this group. One may argue that their values
and assumptions are not necessarily those of people in the
heartland and on the fringes of American society. This ob-
jection would be valid if these plays never circulated beyond
the legitimate theatres of Times Square and the lofts and
cafes of Greenwich Village, but such is obviously not the
case. These plays are usually taken out into the country by
touring companies, performed by provincial theatre groups,
presented at the dinner theatres now enjoying such a vogue,
and made available to mass audiences in television and mo-
tion picture versions. Their general dissemination throughout the entire society argues for their wide appeal.

The five awards whose winners comprise the basis
for this study are not the only drama prizes awarded in this

country, but they are, I believe, a representative group. The Pulitzer Prize is the oldest, best known, and most conservative of the group. The Village Voice Off-Broadway Award (The Obie) represents the other end of the spectrum, concerned as it is with plays exhibiting experimental techniques and presenting daring and unconventional themes. The Drama Critics' Circle Award, established in the 1930's to rectify errors in critical judgment made by Pulitzer jurors who, the Circle critics contended, were often either timid or tasteless, is primarily concerned with artistic merit. The Antoinette Perry Award (The Tony) is primarily drawn to commercial successes, at least according to Robert Brustein. Included for balance is the Players' Workshop Award, a prize given to serious plays originating in the provincial theatres. Taken altogether, the plays which won one of these five awards provide a broad sample of popular American drama.

The themes I have chosen to consider all center on man's most perennial and universal concerns: his relationships to his family, his vocation, his society, and his God. Chapter 1 explores the American attitude toward love and marriage. It focuses on "Women and Marriage" in spite of the obvious fact that wherever there is a married woman there is also a married man, because in drama as in life, marriage is usually (for better or worse) the pivotal event in a woman's life, as assumption less often made by men. Chapter 2 discusses the attitudes expressed about work, material rewards, and the idea of a successful life--in short, the American dream. Chapter 3 forms a bridge between the personal and the wider social context. It concentrates on attitudes toward violence, both individual aggression and mass violence or war. Chapter 4 is concerned with man's relationship to the state and examines statements the plays make about American government, politics, and politicians. Finally, Chapter 5 asks what popular American drama says about man's relationship to God, especially in terms of orthodox religious beliefs. Obviously, other themes could have been explored (can be explored is perhaps a better statement of the subject), but these five chapters provide, it is hoped, a fairly comprehensive (and sometimes surprising) view of the American value system.

Several caveats are perhaps in order at this point. First, this study does not attempt a complete summary of any play, nor does it discuss the play's critical reception or its accumulated scholarship. I have argued elsewhere that such information would be useful and have made it available in a bibliographical and descriptive guide, Prize-Winning Drama in America (1973). Furthermore, this study does not provide complete analyses of plays, nor are the themes of separate dramas necessarily explored. It is not the function of this study to offer a "teaching aid" for a single play, but rather to make some observations about the assumptions made by all of America's prize-winning dramatists. Some plays receive detailed treatment in more than one chapter; others are merely mentioned in passing; a few not useful to my purposes are neglected entirely. In brief, this study feels no compulsion to give "equal time" to every play that won one or more of these prizes. Moreover, the method used in this study is largely impressionistic. It seemed to me, after reading these eighty or so plays, that taken altogether they made certain assumptions about and gave certain insights into American culture. I did not plod mechanically back through every play in search of any chance references to my subject. Therefore, there are certain to be lines here, speeches there, perhaps even a whole play, which would qualify one of my arguments.

I should like here to acknowledge the help of those who made this work possible. Gratitude is due Drs. Milton Rickles and Frank Meriwether, both of the University of Southwestern Louisiana English department, for their careful reading of the manuscript. I want also to thank Margaret Simpson and Sylvia Larson for their assistance with the typing. I am finally particularly grateful to Dr. Paul T. Nolan, Dupré Professor of Humanities at the University of Southwestern Louisiana, who suggested the need for such a study and who provided constant encouragement and practical assistance.

Chapter 1

WOMEN AND MARRIAGE

In 1923 Arthur Hobson Quinn, in commenting on <u>To</u>
<u>the Ladies</u>!, a sentimental comedy by George S. Kaufman
and Marc Connelly, reflected the common, educated opinion
about the "new American drama" and the subject of women
and marriage. According to Professor Quinn, a play like
<u>To the Ladies</u>! which treated marriage "without malice, with-
out bitterness, with reticence and with sympathy," was "near-
er truth" and therefore "better art" than plays with critical
reputations because it showed woman in her proper role as
wife and homemaker and because it demonstrated that only a
woman who accepted her role as subordinate to her husband
could find happiness. Such a play, in Quinn's view, was
"worth a dozen morbid analyses of mismated couples...."[1]
Back of Quinn's comment are several assumptions.
First, he suggests that the highest critical acclaim--that
which is reflected in the granting of drama awards--often
goes to plays which encourage a disrespect for marriage and
call upon women to revolt against the role of homemaker.[2]
Although he points out that feminism was "in the air," his
remarks suggest that the natural role for women is that of
homemaker and helpmeet. Finally, he implies that although
the institution has become a "target of attack" in serious
American plays, marriage is naturally a happy state.
As a matter of fact, the play he praises--<u>To the</u>

1

Ladies!--is, in some respects, a satiric comment upon the
unfairness of marriage to women. It is true, however, that
Kaufmann and Connelly do assume that an intelligent woman
can find happiness inside marriage, and their play suggests
that she will find it nowhere else.

Judging from the treatment of women and marriage in
the seventy-seven plays awarded serious drama prizes from
1917 to 1970, however, one would need to make serious qualifications in Quinn's first assumption. It is true that in many
plays the state of marriage is viewed unfavorably. The first
Pulitzer Prize-winning play, Why Marry?, for example, poses
the question whether marriage is not a worn-out institution in
itself. Such later plays as Street Scene, Who's Afraid of Virginia Woolf? and A Delicate Balance do, it is also true, show
marriages that are unhappy. In prize-winning play after
prize-winning play, moreover, women, and men too, are
shown as victims of their mates and of marriage.

In spite of such evidence, however, the prize-winning
plays, almost without exception, accept Professor Quinn's
assumptions about the nature of women and the necessity of
marriage to their happiness. If one were to view the American woman and marriage solely from the evidence of these
seventy-seven prize-winning plays, he would have to conclude
that although some men should not marry, most women
should; that although some marriages are unhappy, .there is,
as Samuel Johnson once commented, no salvation for women
outside marriage; and that, in the final analysis, the wise
woman will sacrifice everything, even personal integrity, for
her marriage. Back of this assumption, of course, is an
attitude toward women (one shared even by the female playwrights) concerning a woman's talents and needs and her relationships to men.

Many plays suggest, of course, that men as well as women live better lives if they marry. The ancient idea that marriage is a good way to settle a wild bachelor down is enunciated by no less august a character than "de Lawd" in Marc Connelly's The Green Pastures,[3] and reiterated in Arthur Miller's Death of a Salesman when Biff, confused, broke, and restless, says, "I'm mixed up very bad. Maybe I ought to get married."[4] In fact, one critic sees the failure of Biff and Happy to marry as a sign of the "sterility and disharmony" of their lives.[5] Owen Davis' Icebound[6] is another play which leads the audience to believe that the marriage of a young ne'er-do-well to a steady, capable girl will effect his redemption. In the final line of the play, one character says of the proposed union, "marriage changes folks-- and any change in him will be a big improvement" (228).

Even though some plays imply that married men flourish while single ones languish, a comparison of these plays with ones treating the single woman is revealing. Plays which show marriage as important to single men are fewer in number, for one thing, but more significant is their striking difference in tone. They lack the sense of desperation so conspicuous in plays which center around the plight of the unmarried woman. Few men grovel on their knees before women, weeping and pleading "please marry me," as Rosemary Sydney does before Howard, her reluctant suitor in Picnic.[7] Few mothers scheme as hard as Amanda Wingfield does in The Glass Menagerie, to get their sons married off. Not many plays show, as Night of the Iguana does, that marriage (or some sort of permanent relationship) is imperative for a man's survival. There is no male equivalent to the cry which female characters have sent echoing through the American theatre for generations: "I don't want to be an old maid."

In the plays dealing with single women, however, the assumption is entirely different. In fact, the winner in 1917 of the first Pulitzer Prize for drama, Jesse Lynch Williams' comedy Why Marry?, states explicitly what most later plays either imply or assume: namely, that for women, there is no viable alternative to marriage. Ironically, many people considered this play a shocking polemic against marriage, but Williams himself explained that his play aimed merely to scrape "the slush of sentimentality and the scum of hypocrisy from our most ancient and necessary institution.... "[8]

Helen, the heroine of Why Marry?, an emancipated career woman of twenty-nine, stands out as one of the two or three competent, independent, and happy single women in prize-winning American plays. Although her conventional sister-in-law calls her a "sexless freak with a scientific degree, " Helen is not only beautiful and desirable, but, unlike the other women in the play, she also commands her own destiny. Her younger sister Jean, on the other hand, exemplifies the powerlessness of the single woman unprepared to support herself and "brought up to be married and nothing else. " Jean must depend on the charity of her domineering brother John, who regards her as an animated chattel he can trade off to a rich man in return for a connection with a socially prominent family. Her choice, as she explains it, is to "live on the bounty of a disapproving brother or a man I do not love!"[9] Helen's only difficulty, however, stems from her having fallen in love with Ernest Hamilton, the brilliant young doctor with whom she works.

Ernest and Helen love and are committed to each other, but like Mirabel and Millamant in Congreve's The Way of the World, they have grave reservations about entering into marriage. That their fears are amply justified, the other characters are designed to prove. John and his wife Lucy, for example, have the same kind of marriage which Jean and her rich suitor Rex are about to contract, one in which the wife, a legalized prostitute, exchanges her soul and body for a confining arrangement providing nothing more than security and respectability. Uncle Everette is divorcing his wife after twenty-five years of stultifying boredom, and Uncle Theodore, a poor clergyman, the only happily married member of the group, finds he must compromise his principles in order to keep his large family together after the collapse of his wife from overwork. Helen and Ernest are understandably skittish about joining the ranks of these miserable people whose wretched marriages, as Quinn observes, secure sympathy for Helen and Ernest's point of view. [10]

Helen, furthermore, does not wish to give up her career to become a household drudge, nor does she want to hamper Ernest's promising future. Finally, both Helen and Ernest find signing a contract distasteful, and both regard the marriage ceremony itself as "medieval gibberish." Helen, having decided that marriage is burdensome to the husband and demeaning to the wife, casts about for an alternative, and to everyone's horror (especially Ernest's) suggests that they simply agree to belong to each other without any legal arrangement. Although the union she proposes-- one in which they will live apart, have no children, continue their medical research together, and impose upon each other the least possible number of restrictions--has a puritanical ring, the entire family convulses with shame at the very idea.

The play ends with that hoary stage device, the trick

marriage. The reluctant bride and groom, annoyed at first,
decide to let matters stand. Their objections to marriage
are still unanswered, but presumably they realize that all
other solutions are unworkable and accept the thematic statement of the play as intoned by Uncle Everette: "Marriage
is in a bad way, but it's the less of two evils."[11]

That marriage represents the lesser of two evils was
to become one of the most pervasive themes in prize-winning
American plays, but Why Marry? is unique in that its protagonist has a range of choices. Helen's independence, which
protects her from being bullied into marrying a man she
does not love, and her career, which provides her with a
workable alternative should she decide not to marry the man
she does love, give her perhaps the most commanding position of any woman in this group of plays. Most women in
American drama are far less fortunate. Helen, at one point
in the play, tells Jean that one should only marry a man
when one "simply can't live without him."[12] Coming from a
woman in Helen's position, the remark is romantic and hy-
perbolic; to the women who follow, it becomes the literal
truth. They marry to survive.

The life of the single woman is depicted in these
plays as a life of horrors. Victimized, preyed upon, ex-
ploited, forced to eat the bitter bread of charity, they marry
in desperation, usually making matches which virtually guarantee their unhappiness, but which at least make them invul-
nerable to the indignities visited upon the spinster. Again
and again, these plays insist that marriage, to any man and
under any conditions, is better than none. Especially during the twenties and early thirties, a period when many women were questioning whether a life exclusively preoccupied
with home and family was necessary or desirable,[13] the im-

portant plays seemed to assume that salvation for women
could be found only in marriage, even an unhappy one.

Miss Lulu Bett, [14] by Zona Gale, the Pulitzer winner
for 1920-21, was the first prize-winning play to explore the
plight of the single woman and the improbability of making
a decent life outside of marriage.   Lulu Bett is a thirty-
three year old maiden lady who lives on the charity of her
sister and brother-in-law, Ina and Dwight Deacon.   An un-
paid servant in their household whom they alternately ridicule and patronize, Lulu is supposedly rescued by her marriage to Dwight's brother Ninian.   Like Helen and Ernest in
Why Marry?, they are tricked into marriage and decide to
acquiesce.   Lulu's happiness is short-lived, however, for
Ninian, on the wedding trip, confesses he was previously
married to a woman he now presumes is dead.   Lulu, await-
ing clarification, reluctantly goes back to Dwight and Ina.
Although their household has all but collapsed in her absence,
the Deacons are not happy to see her return.   They now
consider her a fallen woman and fear a scandal should
Ninian turn out to be a bigamist.   When Lulu, whose spine
has been stiffened by her marriage, refuses to tell the
neighbors that Ninian left her because they were incompatible,
Dwight orders her out.   With no means of support and only
twelve dollars to her name, Lulu prepares to depart.

In the play's original ending, Ninian's first wife turns
up alive, leaving Lulu to face an uncertain future alone, but
when playgoers clamored for a "happy ending," Miss Gale,
bowing to public taste, supplied a new act in which Ninian
and Lulu learn of the first wife's death in time for a routine embrace at the final curtain. [15]   The audience's assumption that Lulu's marriage constitutes a happy ending is revealing, for it ignores the unlovely picture the play paints of

that institution. The Deacons, for example, have a completely vacuous relationship, and the child of their union
ranks among the most monstrous in American dramatic literature. The Deacon's older daughter, in spite of what she
has seen of marriage, nearly elopes with a boy she does
not love, merely to escape her family. Her desire to escape parallels Lulu's except that Lulu has some affection
for Ninian, the agent of her release. Lulu knows, however,
that she loves Ninian only because he was the first person
ever to pay her any attention, and she admits that she could
just as easily have married someone else. Ninian seems a
kind man and a good prospect, except that he has already
been unhappily married once. The most devastating indictment of marriage, however, comes from Lulu's mother.
When asked whether Lulu will not be better off married than
single, she replies that it won't make much difference. She
says that although she has had a husband and six children,
her life seems as empty as Lulu's. Lulu, in fact, has an
advantage, according to her mother, because she "ain't had
the pain" (119). As Lulu is about to leave the Deacons with
no prospects, Mother Bett says that at least she will be
able "to call her soul her own."

Lulu's future without marriage would be grim indeed,
but in view of the misogamist undercurrents in the play, the
"happy ending" is a qualified one. A pleasant prison and a
gentle jailor are the best a woman in Lulu's position can
expect. Being independent, being a woman who can "call
her soul her own" is a possibility the play never seriously
explores. When Ninian asks Lulu why she has endured the
galling arrangement at the Deacons' for so long, she explains simply that she is trapped. "Women like me," she
tells him, "can't do any other work" (117). Unable to sup-

port herself, she must, like Jean in <u>Why Marry?</u>, settle for
whatever comes her way or live on grudging relatives. Although Arthur Hobson Quinn sees the play as evidence that
the "feminine revolt has not been limited to those under the
yoke of wedlock, "[16] the play does not show a revolt, but
merely an exchange of yokes. Fortunately for Lulu, the
signs are that Ninian's yoke will be light, and if her marriage does not make her happy, at least it will save her
from the horrors of the spinster's life. Her observation
may tell her that marriages are not made in heaven, but her
experience assures her that the lot of the single woman is
hell.

Another play which presupposes the inability of a woman to survive outside of marriage is Eugene O'Neill's
<u>Anna Christie</u>, the Pulitzer Prize winner in 1921-22.
Anna, like Lulu Bett, was, in her youth, a servant in the
house of relatives. After her seduction by one of her cous-
ins, Anna flees the farm for a job as a nursemaid in the
city. Here she hopes to find a suitable husband, but when
she realizes that the men she meets have only dishonorable
intentions, she drifts into a house of prostitution. Finally,
physically and emotionally exhausted, she agrees to join her
father whom she has not seen since childhood. Old Chris,
now the captain of a coal barge, is unaware that his daughter
is a prostitute and takes her to live on his boat. After
several months of fresh air, solitude, and fatherly affection,
Anna is restored to health. Her salvation seems certain
when Mat Burke, a vigorous Irish seaman, meets and falls
in love with her. Mat, who views marriage as a reforming
institution in which he will give up loose women and settle
down with a "dacent" girl (the double standard of morality
is a feature of many of these plays), becomes violently angry

when Anna confesses her sordid past.   Finally, after forcing
Anna to swear on a crucifix that she never loved another
man, Mat agrees to marry her.   The play ends ambiguously,
as it seems highly unlikely that a reformed prostitute and a
puritanical Irish Catholic can be happy together.   According
to O'Neill himself, who wished to stress the tenuousness of
the solution, the "happy ending is merely the comma at the
end of a gaudy introductory clause, the body of the sentence
still unwritten."[17]   One thing appears certain, however;
marriage is Anna's last hope.

Another variation on this theme occurs in Sidney
Howard's Pulitzer winner of 1924-25, They Knew What They
Wanted, a modern interpretation of the classical Paolo and
Francesca story.   In this play, Tony Patucci, a sixty-year
old California wine grower of Italian descent, falls in love,
à la distance, with Amy, a waitress in San Francisco.   Hoping to win her hand, he sends, instead of a photograph of
himself, one of his handsome young foreman, Joe.   Joe also
writes the love letters (Tony's command of the language is
not very good) which convince Amy to accept the proposal
of marriage.

The notion that marriage to anyone is better than
being single is given another twist when Amy arrives to dis-
cover that the bridegroom is not Joe but an old man who
speaks broken English and has two broken legs (the result of
an automobile accident on the way to meet the bride's train).
Amy, appalled by this turn of events, considers calling off
the wedding until she remembers that her only alternative
is to return to the city (in which all the men have dishonorable intentions) and her old job.   Ironically, in spite of this
inauspicious beginning, and in spite of the fact that Amy becomes pregnant by Joe, an incident which, as Arthur Hobson

Quinn observes, somehow escapes being sordid, [18] Amy and
Tony find happiness.   They are, in fact, one of the few con-
tented couples in this body of plays, but their happiness is
the result of Tony's decency and Amy's determination to be
a good wife to the man who saved her.   What is most significant here, however, is Amy's assumption that marriage
to a total stranger, an old and sick one at that, is prefer-
able to being single.

      The next season's Pulitzer Prize winner was Craig's
Wife by George Kelly. [19]   This play also explores the necessity for a woman to find security through marriage; in fact,
the protagonist's drive for that security is so extreme that
it distorts her personality and makes her grotesque.   To
Harriet Craig, brought up in the humiliating position of poor
relation, marriage to a man of comfortable means is not
enough to slake her thirst for a safeguard.   She needs tangi-
ble proof of her invulnerability in the form of a large house
which she maintains with the fanatic fastidiousness of a museum curator.   She needs, moreover, to insure that the
house will always stand between her and the outside world.
To this end, she schemes to get complete control of her
husband Walter, a kind, romantic man with little conception
of her machinations.

      Actually, what Harriet prizes most, even more than
an affluent husband, is complete independence, a luxury she
cannot afford.   Unlike most women in these plays, who will-
ingly sacrifice their autonomy for a safe haven, Harriet
plans to have both by reducing Walter to as negligible a fact-
or as his passiveness and gullibility will permit.   She will
not settle for less than the "independence of authority, " as
she calls it, over the man she married.

      A good deal of Harriet's philosophy of marriage is re-

vealed early in the play through a conversation with her
niece Ethel, a girl considering marriage to a penniless college professor.   Ethel's mother, seriously ill and anxious to
have Ethel settled, approves the match, but Harriet expresses surprise, not only that Ethel wants to marry a poor
man, but that she should care to marry at all.   "Why, " she
asks Ethel, who stands to inherit her mother's money,
"should a person need anybody, dear, if he has enough to
get along on?" (325).   When Ethel tries to explain that she
loves the young man, Harriet scornfully dismisses romantic
love as "impractical" and "mere sentimentality. "   To surrender to it, Harriet warns, is to risk reverting to "the almost primitive feminine dependence and subjection" that women "have been struggling to emancipate themselves from
for centuries" (326).

The play comes to its crisis when Walter, his eyes
finally opened, accuses Harriet of exploiting him to insure
her personal safety.   In her own defense, she explains that
she was merely trying to preserve her home.   "What else
has a woman like me but a home?" she cries.   When Walter
reminds her that she has a husband, she replies that a woman always stands to lose both the husband and the home,
unless she never lets "control of them get out of her hands"
(362).   Walter, revolted by his wife's mercenary vision of
their marriage, decides to leave, and the play ends with
Harriet, deserted by everyone, wandering desolately about
the great house.

Harriet's ruthless calculations, her contempt for the
non-utilitarian values, and her inability to love and trust a
good man insure that her exposure and defeat are justified
and satisfying to the audience, which incidentally, cheered
wildly when Walter finally rebelled. [20]   Although Harriet is

an unattractive character, she is not one of unmotivated malignancy.   Behind her obsessive fears lies a first-hand understanding of the powerlessness of the woman alone.   Her mother loved and trusted her father explicitly, and he repaid her by mortgaging the "home over her head" for another wo- man.   After her mother's death, Harriet lived twelve years under her stepmother's roof and five years with a married sister.   "I know what it is," she says, "to be on someone else's floor."   Unlike Ethel, she has no private fortune and no special equipment for supporting herself "outside of a few more or less inapplicable college theories."   Why her college education did not prepare her for independence the play never explains.   At any rate, marriage was her last resort, and although she recognizes that Walter is a good man, she can never feel secure, for the protection she craves is based on "the mood of a man," the husband, "the lord and master," as she explains to Ethel.   Behind Har- riet's militant avarice lies a haunting dread of being aban- doned and cast adrift in a world where a woman with no money and no man is always vulnerable.   The play points up the problems spawned by a relationship in which women are economically dependent on men; in fact, according to Eleanor Flexner, neither Marx nor Engels expounded "the cash nexus as the basis of modern marriage more explicitly than it is voiced here."[21]   Harriet's trickery and hardness of heart are repellent, but she has been trapped by forces she can- not control, a fact which the playwright fails to recognize in spite of the fact that Montrose Moses argued he had the best understanding of "feminine human nature" since Clyde Fitch.[22]

Although the idea that women need marriage to sur- vive receives its greatest emphasis during the twenties and early thirties, the theme has reappeared many times since.

William Saroyan's play The Time of Your Life, winner of
the 1939-40 Pulitzer Prize, for example, features the pathetic Kitty Duval, whose marriage saves her from a sordid life
as a waterfront prostitute.   Tom, the man she marries, is
somewhat simple, but he has a heart of gold (like hers),
and the play holds up their marriage as the solution to her
problems.   The play suggests, in Winifred Dusenbury's view,
that their union could "elevate and purify" the girl who had
formerly been "spiritually crippled. "23

        An example of a woman destroyed because she has no
protector is Blanche DuBois, protagonist of Tennessee Williams' Streetcar Named Desire, which won both the Pulitzer
Prize and the Drama Critics' Circle Award for 1947-48.
Blanche has been severely neurotic since the death of her
husband, a homosexual who killed himself when Blanche dis-
covered his relationship with another man.   She is now
stretched out on the rack of the dependent single woman, for
the spinster is, as Robert Emmet Jones observes, the "most
pathetic and ill-treated being in the South. "24   Reduced to
accepting the unwilling charity of her brutish brother-in-law
Stanley Kowalski, she hopes to find protection and security
through marriage to Mitch, one of Stanley's poker-playing
friends.   Although Blanche would have considered Mitch her
social inferior in her palmy days, he is more than acceptable now that she has lost the family plantation, lost her job
as a teacher, and been hounded out of town for promiscuity.
Unfortunately for Blanche, Stanley, in an act of manly solidarity, ruins her chances for marriage by telling Mitch
about her past.   After the destruction of her hopes and after
her brutal rape by Stanley, Blanche's tenuous hold on her
sanity snaps.

        A few plays do go beyond the question of economic

and social survival to show that women need marriage emotionally or spiritually to complete themselves, to achieve
their "manifest destiny, " as it were.   The central character
of Zoe Akins' The Old Maid (Pulitzer Prize, 1934-35) stood
as a warning to the unmarried women of the audience, which
Burns Mantle called as "heavily feminine" as the play itself. [25]   In her youth, Charlotte committed an indiscretion
with a young painter and secretly had a child, whose up-
bringing she supervised from a distance.   Because Charlotte
never married, the child was reared in her cousin's household, became devoted to the woman and even called her
"Mama. "   Charlotte, embittered by her life as an old maid
and galled at seeing her daughter brought up by someone
else, declines into a sour and unattractive old woman.

Perhaps the play which presents most vividly the idea
that women must marry to find happiness is the Pulitzer
Prize winner for 1927-28, Eugene O'Neill's Strange Interlude,
a play which Edward Engel calls a modern "every-woman. "[26]
The play is a nine-act extravaganza, all nine of which suggest that the role of women is to give themselves to men,
to live through men, and to bear children.   The play begins
with the struggle of Nina Leeds to rebuild her life after her
fiance dies in the war.   In an attempt to atone for not having "given herself" to her lover before he went away, Nina,
hovering on the edge of a mental breakdown, "gives herself"
promiscuously to soldiers in the Veterans' hospital where
she works.   The familiar idea that marriage solves personal problems is introduced when Nina's doctor and friend,
Ned Darrell, promotes her marriage to Sam Evans, a naive
boy who the doctor thinks will make a stable and suitable
husband.   The prescription seems to work, and Nina improves rapidly, especially after she finds she is to have a

child. Unfortunately, however, she learns from Sam's
mother of hereditary insanity in the Evans family and without Sam's ever knowing of her pregnancy, secretly has an
abortion.

Nina assumes it is her duty to bear her husband a
child, particularly since Sam, thinking himself sterile, becomes apathetic and depressed. Finally, Nina appeals to
Ned to father a child, which he, ostensibly in the interest of
his patient's welfare, is only too willing to do. Predictably,
they fall in love, but when Ned asks Nina to go away with
him, she declines, for she now has a coterie of adoring
males: Sam, Ned, her infant son, and Marsden, a Prufrockian character she has known since childhood. The re-
mainder of the play concerns the complex interaction of Nina
with these four men. She never finds the fulfillment she so
intensely seeks, settling instead for peace with Marsden.
Significantly, however, her search never goes beyond this
tissue of relationships.

Nina, unlike the passive, supine women in many of
these plays, has been able to transcend the trade of self for
security and shelter; yet she is as trapped as any of them
because she defines herself in relation to men. She can
only think of herself as Sam's wife, Ned's mistress, Gor-
don's mother. Nina has only two moments of intense happiness: when she feels her child move in her womb, and
again when she senses her possession of the four males.
Although she is intelligent and sophisticated, in control of
her life for the most part, she has no vision of herself outside her hysterical absorption in personal relationships. In
many ways, her life is even more limited than that of the
two spinsters in Lillian Hellman's Toys in the Attic (Circle
winner, 1959-60), who fasten upon their brother Julian, liv-

ing for him and through him with a devouring and parasitic
intensity, ruining his life with their "unthinkingly possessive"
brand of loving. [27]   But they also work, learn French, plan
trips abroad; Nina, on the other hand, devotes the entire
sum of her energy to the men who are apparently essential
to her definition of herself as a person.   The exclusive pre-
occupation with intense and convoluted personal relationships
gives Strange Interlude the fetid atmosphere of the soap
opera, a kind of "Nina Faces Life, " as one wag put it.

          Unlike Nina, many women in these plays cry out for
a wider life and for the freedom traditionally reserved for
the male.   If they do not surrender such ideas immediately,
recognizing them as alien to their best interests, someone,
usually a man, will remind them that their real chance for
happiness lies not in the pursuit of their own development,
but rather in the functions of wife and mother.   Perhaps
nowhere is this more clearly shown that in Jan de Hartog's
Tony winner, The Fourposter (1951-52), a play which centers
around the married life of Michael, a writer, and his wife
Agnes, and is, according to Brooks Atkinson, the story "in
cameo" of all marriages. [28]   After the departure of their
last child from the nest, Agnes shows signs of restlessness.
Finally, tired of existing in Michael's shadow and eager for
one last chance to be her own person, Agnes announces her
intention to leave.   Michael suspects that the vacuum in
Agnes' life was created when her job of mothering ended,
leaving her vulnerable to romantic nonsense.   He therefore
hastens to assure her that she is his sole inspiration.   Once
she understands that she is central to Michael's life, Agnes
puts away any ideas of a life of her own.

          While the bulk of prize-winning plays insist with mo-
notonous regularity that women must marry, a small number

do offer a minority view. A few suggest, for example, that
marriage may not suit women of exceptional talent and extraordinary dedication. This idea is presented in Why Marry?,
in which both Helen, a talented scientist, and her fiance fear
that marriage will cut short her promising career, turning
her into "a superior servant in an inferior household."
Celia Copplestone, a woman of unusual spirituality and
strength in T. S. Eliot's play The Cocktail Party (Tony
Award, 1949-50), is advised to take the high road--the life
of a single person devoted to the service of God. Mediocre
souls like Edward and Lavinia, on the other hand, are encouraged to seek some measure of happiness within the
mundane limits of married life. [29]

One play alone stands in sharp contrast to all the
rest by condemning marriage regardless of a woman's situation. Elmer Rice's Street Scene, the Pulitzer Prize winner
for 1928-29, presents liberal views about women and their
role which represent the minority opinion even today. [30] The
play shows the growing awareness of a young girl, Rose
Maurrant, that marriage, even to a kind and loving man,
may be a mistake. She learns from observing her mother's
life, that marriages are often restrictive, requiring women
to subordinate their emotional needs and deny their feelings.
After Rose's father shoots her mother, leaving Rose to look
after her younger brother, Rice provides the standard solution to her problem. Sam Kaplan, a young law student in
the same tenement, proposes marriage, but Rose declines
his offer, explaining that "people ought not belong to anybody
but themselves" (596). When Sam asks if she plans to go
through life alone, never loving anyone, she replies that loving and belonging are not the same thing. She insists that
if her parents had not always depended on others for "what

they ought to have had inside themselves" (596), the tragedy
would have been avoided.

Thus Street Scene, unlike most plays in this group,
says that the way to fulfillment, for both women and men,
is through independence and inner strength.   Only when one
can rely upon himself, can he enter into decent relationships
with others.   Although the play makes a strong case against
marriage and is a strong feminist statement as well, it
does not suggest an alternative for Rose.   It does not explain how Rose, with a brother to support, can survive on
her small wages as a secretary, but it does show that what
she has seen of marriage, in her family and in the tenement
where she lives, has convinced her that marriage can be a
good deal worse than insecurity or even poverty.   Like Ib-
sen's A Doll's House, however, the play merely states the
problem without providing answers.

Such a vision of the limitations women accept in these
plays would be dismal even if the marriages they make out
of necessity made them happy, but as Quinn complained,
marriage in the serious drama is usually grim.   Indeed,
the bleakness of marriage is an important theme in these
plays, and one can very nearly count the happy families on
the fingers of one hand: Amy and Tony in Sidney Howard's
They Knew What They Wanted; Pa Vanderhof's eccentric
brood in the George Kaufman-Moss Hart comedy You Can't
Take It With You;[31] the families in Wilder's Our Town; the
Roosevelts in Dore Schary's Sunrise at Campobello (which
does not touch upon Franklin's adultery or Eleanor's misery);[32] and the couple in Tad Mosel's All the Way Home. [33]
Many plays are concluded with wedding bells and lead one to
assume that the couple will be happy, but of those plays
which actually treat married life, few show the institution

as conducive to the happiness of either husband or wife. In
fact, some of the most celebrated American plays--Cat on a
Hot Tin Roof, [34] Long Day's Journey into Night, [35] and Who's
Afraid of Virginia Woolf?, [36] to mention only three--drama-
tize the seemingly endless varieties of marital wretchedness.
Admittedly, miserable families are richer in dramatic possibilities than happy ones which, as Tolstoy observed, [37]
tend to be all alike.

In some of the plays that depict unhappy marriages,
the woman becomes the dominant partner and victimizes the
husband. Such is the situation in Craig's Wife, Abe Lincoln
in Illinois, The Shrike (perhaps the most extreme example),
and Look Homeward, Angel. In most of these plays, however, the women are thwarted or pay a great price in order
to subordinate themselves to their mates. For Stella Kowalski, Blanche's sister in Streetcar Named Desire by Tennessee
Williams, for example, the price for security and sexual
ecstasy with Stanley is an acceptance of his values and a
denial or repression of her own. As Blanche observes,
civilization has swept on, but Stella wants to "hang back with
the brutes."[38]

Agnes, the wife in Edward Albee's A Delicate Balance,
is characterized as a strong woman who accommodates herself to her weaker husband, deliberately bending to Tobias'
will and repressing her natural executive tendencies. Her
notion of marriage is that the husband makes (or fails to
make) the decisions; the wife accepts the results and goes on
from there. Agnes vents her frustrations on Tobias by di-
recting at him a constant stream of irony and by reminding
him when things get in a muddle that he chose the route; she
merely drove the team. Although John Gassner complained
that Agnes' reproaches appear "unwarranted by the objective

realities of the play, " it seems reasonable to assume that
her acerbity is the price both pay for her passiveness. [39]

Arthur Miller's play Death of a Salesman, while it
does not deal primarily with the problem of marriage, also
shows a wife who conforms to the conventional notion that a
woman should subordinate herself to her husband's judgment,
even when that judgment is bad. Linda has a better developed moral sense than her husband Willy, yet she almost
encourages his mad fantasies and remains silent as he warps
the lives of their sons. Linda is, in many ways, the American ideal of the perfect wife--quiet, docile, devoted, self-
effacing, and fiercely loyal--but she has, like Stella, deferred to a husband who is her moral inferior. As Winifred
Dusenbury observes, Linda is finally alienated from Willy
"because she knows no way to get along except to give in
to him. "[40]

Although some plays assign blame for unhappiness to
either the husband or the wife, others show that marriage
is a hopeless condition for which neither partner is responsible. The two plays by Frank Gilroy, Who'll Save the Plowboy? and The Subject Was Roses, for example, are studies
in frustration caused by marriage. In his comedy The Only
Game in Town, Gilroy has a character describe marriage
as a "feeble and wheezing institution, " but he marries anyway (it's the only game in town). That remark character-
izes the marriages in his two prize-winning plays perfectly.
Gerald Weales, in fact, in discussing Gilroy's treatment of
marriage, says his plays exhibit a "sense of things as bleak
as that in Albee. "[41]

Perhaps the play which most solidly sustains the
image of marriage as the spoiler of hopes is Eugene O'Neill's
Beyond the Horizon, [42] the Pulitzer Prize play of 1919-20.

This play concerns two brothers, Robert and Andrew, and
Ruth, the girl they both love. Robert, a dreamy idealist,
longs to go to sea, while Andrew, a more stolid type, plans
to marry Ruth and run the family farm. When Ruth reveals
that she loves Robert, Andrew ships out, while Robert marries and tries to become a farmer. Predictably, he fails
and loses the respect of his wife. Desperately unhappy that
he gave up his chance to explore the world for a "narrow
prison, " he is glad to escape his cramped and misspent life
through death. Andrew, too, has been corrupted. Where
he once lived contentedly in a creative partnership with nature, his travels have made him a materialist and a gambler.
As for Ruth, her disillusionment makes her sadistic at first,
then leaves her utterly incapable of feeling.

Although Arthur Hobson Quinn says that Ruth ruined
the lives of both men, [43] the culprit is romantic love, which
causes the characters to make the wrong choices. Ruth
and Andrew could have made a reasonably happy marriage
because they share the same temperament and values. Ironically, the very qualities which attract Ruth to Robert--his
sensitivity, his dreamy and poetic nature--are the very traits
which unsuit him for marriage and farming. The play further deflates the concept of romantic love when Robert's
uncle, a sea captain, says he cannot understand how Robert
could let "a little huggin' and kissin' " (70) stand in the way
of his making a man of himself. When Andrew confesses
later that he recovered from that "kid idea" (loving Ruth)
after six months at sea, romantic love becomes an infantile
disease.

If this group of prize-winning plays reflects common-
ly held attitudes in America, one can only conclude that the
prevailing assessment of women and their potential for self-

realization and autonomy is rather low. The message, over
and over, conscious and unconscious, stated and implied, is
that women are destined for lives of parasitic attachments
and vicarious pleasures. While the picture is not uniformly
grim--one can find a few artists, a scientist, a teacher or
two and Eleanor Roosevelt in these plays--for the majority,
wedding, bedding and breeding are the limits. Because they
have been denied a place in the world's arena, or because
they have had no vision of themselves in it,[44] they take
refuge in marriages which often leave them vaguely dissatis-
fied if not frankly wretched. For every Annie Sullivan in
these plays one can think of dozens of unhappy and unproductive women. Marriage is, nevertheless, assumed to be
more desirable than the single life. Most single women here
are objects of pity or ridicule, and few choose the role. In
popular American drama, a woman must either marry or
resign herself to a place at the fringes of life.

The insistance in popular drama upon conventional
marriage values provides an interesting contrast to the popular fiction of the same period. According to one observer,[45]
the stories in the slick women's magazines, at least until
the onset of the "togetherness" era, featured career women
and held up such qualities as courage, independence, and
competence for admiration. W. J. Stuckey, a student of the
Pulitzer Prize novels, reports that the books tapped for that
honor are also filled with heroic and aggressive women who
shake off the role of the passive female to compete success-
fully with men in the arts, in science, and in the market-
place. In fact, the tendency of these novels to glorify women and their achievements prompts Stuckey to brand them
as examples of "middle-class female wish fulfillment."[46]

Why the popular drama should say so emphatically

that woman's place is in the home is intriguing and finally disquieting. Unless one simply dismisses most of the plays as "middle-class male wish fulfillment," he must consider the possibility that the popular drama gives a more accurate reading of American life than popular fiction does. Perhaps American women do want the security marriage provides more than they want freedom. Perhaps the massive retreat into domesticity which followed the social upheavals of the 20's, the uncertainties of the Great Depression, and the hardships of World War II, signaled the return of American women to the role they most want to play--with all of its attendant limitations--that of wife and mother. The reluctance of many women to exercise the options open to them, and the refusal of many to support legislation designed to guarantee their equality (at the expense of their traditional privileges) would support such a hypothesis. If this is so, then the image of women found in the prize-winning plays is closer to the truth than many would want to admit.

NOTES

1.   Arthur Hobson Quinn, Contemporary American Plays
      (New York: Scribner's, 1923), p. xxv.

2.   Ibid., p. xxii.

3.   A New Edition of the Pulitzer Prize Plays, eds.
      Kathryn Coe and William H. Cordell (New York:
      Random House, 1940), p. 614.   All subsequent quo-
      tations from plays are from the editions cited.   Page
      numbers are incorporated in the text.   According to
      Paul T. Nolan, "God on Stage: A Problem in Char-
      acterization in Marc Connelly's The Green Pastures"
      (Xavier University Studies, IX [May, 1965], p. 81),
      the disparity between God and the other characters
      is established in part by His assumption that man's
      life on earth will be simple provided he has a good
      job and a wife.

4. *Masters of Modern Drama,* eds. Haskell Block and
    Robert Shedd (New York: Random House, 1962),
    p. 1023.

5. Richard J. Foster, "Confusion and Tragedy: The Fail-
    ure of Miller's Salesman, " *Two Modern American
    Tragedies: Reviews and Criticism,* ed. John D. Hur-
    rell (New York: Charles Scribner's Sons, 1961),
    p. 85.

6. *A New Edition of the Pulitzer Prize Plays,* pp. 191-
    228.

7. William Inge (New York: Random House, 1953),
    pp. 126-127.

8. Quoted in Arthur Hobson Quinn's *Contemporary Ameri-
    can Plays,* p. 3.

9. *Why Marry?* (New York: Charles Scribner's Sons,
    1914), p. 184.

10. *A History of American Drama from the Civil War to
    the Present Day* (New York: Harper and Bros.,
    1927), II, 71.

11. *Why Marry?,* p. 206.

12. *Ibid.,* p. 23.

13. This trend has been well documented.   For an informal
    review, see Frederick Lewis Allen's *Only Yesterday*
    (New York: Perennial Library, 1964), pp. 80-81.

14. *A New Edition of the Pulitzer Prize Plays,* pp. 105-
    145.

15. John Toohey, *A History of the Pulitzer Prize Plays*
    (New York: Citadel Press, Inc., 1967), p. 21.

16. *Contemporary American Plays,* p. xxvi.

17. *A Treasury of the Theatre,* ed. John Gassner (New
    York: Simon and Schuster, 1950), p. 788.

18. *History of the American Drama,* II, 228-229.

19. *A New Edition of the Pulitzer Prize Plays*, pp. 317-379.

20. John Toohey, p. 51.

21. *American Playwrights: 1918-1938* (New York: Simon and Schuster, 1938), p. 238.

22. *Dramas of Modernism and Their Forerunners* (New York: Little, Brown and Co., 1931), p. 551.

23. *The Theme of Loneliness in Modern American Drama* (Gainesville, Fla.: University of Florida Press, 1960), p. 161.

24. "Tennessee Williams' Early Heroines," *Modern Drama*, II (December, 1959), 214.

25. (New York: Appleton-Century Co., 1934). Burns Mantle's remark, from his review in the *Daily News*, is quoted by John Toohey, p. 127.

26. Engel's description of the play appears in F. I. Carpenter's *Eugene O'Neill* (New York: Twayne Publishers, Inc., 1964), p. 122.

27. See John Gassner's analysis of the play in *Dramatic Soundings* (New York: Crown Publishers, Inc., 1968), pp. 481-484.

28. *Best American Plays, 1951-57*, ed. John Gassner (New York: Crown Publishers, Inc., 1958). Atkinson's remark is quoted by John Gassner in his introduction to the play, p. 480.

29. According to Grover Smith, Jr. in *T. S. Eliot's Poetry and Plays* (Chicago: Univ. of Chicago Press, 1956), Celia and the Chamberlaynes are initiated into vocations according to their potentialities. Edward and Lavinia are incapable of enlightenment, so they must "make the best of a bad job" (p. 225).

30. *A New Edition of the Pulitzer Prize Plays*, pp. 541-597. Basic to the play, for example, is the notion of "the wrongness of one individual's owning another...," according to Frank Durham's *Elmer Rice* (New York: Twayne Publishers, Inc., 1970), p. 66.

31. These people are happily married because they are
    zany. As Eleanor Flexner observes, they are escap-
    ists, having turned their backs on real life. (Ameri-
    can Playwrights, p. 225).

32. Joseph P. Lash's recent study of the Roosevelts, Elea-
    nor and Franklin (New York: W. W. Norton and Co.,
    1971), treats these aspects of their marriage so con-
    spicuously absent in Schary's romanticized version.

33. Even the Follets have areas of conflict between them,
    but as George Oppenheimer (Newsday, Dec. 14, 1960)
    observes, "they are stated rather than explored. "

34. Tennessee Williams, Best American Plays, 1951-57.
    The members of this miserable family all live, as
    Books Atkinson put it, "in solitary confinement" (New
    York Times, April 3, 1955).

35. Eugene O'Neill (New Haven: Yale Univ. Press, 1955).
    Here, according to Doris Falk in her Eugene O'Neill
    and the Tragic Tension (New Brunswick, New Jersey:
    Rutgers Univ. Press, 1958), "each of the protago-
    nists is partly responsible for his own destruction
    and partly a victim of the family fate" (194-195).

36. Edward Albee, Best American Plays, 1957-1963. Har-
    old Lamport, in an essay in The Saturday Review
    (June 29, 1963), describes the relationship of George
    and Martha as "an incredible inferno of sado-maso-
    chism...."

37. Anna Karenina, tr. Constance Garnett (Garden City:
    Doubleday and Co., 1946), p. 2.

38. Streetcar Named Desire, p. 70.

39. Gassner's remark appears in Dramatic Soundings,
    p. 604.

40. Theme of Loneliness in Modern American Drama,
    p. 24.

41. The Jumping-Off Place: American Drama in the 1960's
    (New York: The Macmillan Co., 1969), p. 90.

42. A New Edition of the Pulitzer Prize Plays, pp. 53-104.

43. Contemporary American Plays, p. xviii.

44. Germaine Greer in The Female Eunuch (New York:
    Bantam Books, 1970), suggests that the latter possi-
    bility is more likely than the former. Emancipation
    has failed, in her view, and although "the cage door"
    is open, the canary has "refused to fly out" (2).

45. Betty Friedan, The Feminine Mystique (New York: W.
    W. Norton, 1963), pp. 38-41.

46. The Pulitzer Prize Novels: A Critical Backward Look
    (Norman, Oklahoma: Univ. of Oklahoma Press, 1966),
    p. 214.

Chapter 2

WORK AND MATERIAL REWARDS

When James Truslow Adams in 1931 coined the label "the American Dream"--"that dream of a better, richer and happier life for all our citizens of every rank,"[1] he gave a name to centuries of vague millennial hopes which had finally become centered upon America as the New Eden. Although the American Dream is a shadowy concept, shifting and difficult to define, most observers agree that it is America's most potent myth, "one of the motivating forces of American civilization...."[2] It pervades almost every aspect of American life. The American political structure is based upon it, for the Founding Fathers were inspired by the Dream, and its threads are woven deep into the fabric of the Declaration of Independence and the Bill of Rights.[3] The philosophy of education in this country since Thomas Jefferson derives from this concept, for it is assumed that schools can and should insure equal opportunity.[4] Finally, American art has inevitably been colored and flavored by the idea of this country as the land of opportunity.[5]

At some point in this country's development, however, the energizing dream of a "better, richer and happier life" narrowed down in the minds of many to the simple dream of riches. "Better" and "happier" became synonymous with "richer" in the sense of "wealthier." The notion of America as a place where anyone could get rich, in spite of massive evidence to the contrary, [6] sank deep into the national marrow. Many of the country's prominent men of letters either denied the validity of the dream or proclaimed it a tawdry ideal, many shouted "no in thunder, " excoriated or ridiculed those who lusted after the bitch goddess, but all such protest only testifies to the seemingly inexhaustible vitality of the myth.

In spite of the presence of nay-sayers, [7] literature of the widest popular appeal has usually served up the American Dream uncritically, and the success story, from the parables of Horatio Alger to the philosophy of The Reader's Digest, is a familiar feature of the literary landscape. Alger, whose name is a synonym for success, is remembered (although his stories are not) because his mythic interpretation of the American experience struck a chord. His "simple, but enormously compelling, vision of a fluid society which infallibly rewarded the plucky and lucky with fame and fortune... "[8] captured the national imagination and squared with the way many people wanted to see themselves and the country. Countless people, probably paragons of industry, thrift, and piety, have comforted themselves in their poverty with sentimental Algerism, sustained by the belief that their hard work would shortly add up to security and respectability. In a country in which many people sincerely believe that any boy could become President, the glorification of the self-made man was perhaps inevitable.

Certainly Alger's "rags-to-riches" theme has not been confined to those books which have made his name a household word. It has become one of the most pervasive themes in American literature, and novels which assume that virtue and hard work equal material rewards can be found at al-

most every level of literary sophistication. Indeed, according to W. J. Stuckey's study of the Pulitzer Prize novels,
the qualities most often celebrated in these books are "self-
reliance, industriousness, and acquisitiveness." For Pulitzer judges, Stuckey concludes, "the highest standard of
American manners and manhood" is little more than "sublimated greed."[9]

The view of the success ethic reflected in the most
popular American drama, plays which have won major awards
for drama since 1917, is nowhere so consistent as Stuckey
finds it in the Pulitzer Prize novels. While few plays deny
that America is the land of opportunity, many are frankly
skeptical about the process of getting rich, and few place at
the highest level of virtue those who have lifted themselves
by their bootstraps. In fact, a number of these plays insist
upon the corrupting aspects of materialsim; several question
or deny the value of both work and success; some extol the
value of work but not of money. A few, while intending to
confirm the myth, cast doubts upon it; others, while intending to deny it, seem unconsciously to affirm it.

Perhaps the play which presents the myth most com-
pletely and with the least skepticism is Sidney Howard's
Pulitzer Prize-winner of 1924-25, They Knew What They
Wanted.[10] The protagonist and ethical center of the play is
sixty-year old Tony Pattuci, the American Dream come true.
Twenty years before the play begins, Tony had left Italy for
California, where by hard work and good luck (the Volstead
Act) he has become a prosperous wine-grower.

Tony's characterization gives the lie to critics of the
success ethic who see the self-made man as dour, stingy,
obsessive about work, and conservative. Tony has a sunny
disposition, takes a childlike pleasure in having and spending

his money, entertains Mediterranean notions about the proper
balance of work and play: "after festa workin' is more
easy" (282). It is true that his affluence has made him mildly conservative, and he freely admits that he would not like
to see changes in the system that allowed him, even helped
him, to get rich. But when his position is presented vis-a-
vis the noisy radicalism of his foreman Joe, a former I. W.
W. organizer, Tony's philosophy seems the more attractive.
Joe, the reformer, turns out to be merely a drifter, un-
pregnant in his cause, and reluctant to accept responsibility.
In the light of Tony's lavish generosity to Joe and to all of
his employees, Joe's Wobbly songs about cruel bosses seem
absurd. As the play ends, Tony, the man Joe had contemptuously branded a "bloomin' Capitalist" (307), proves
himself Joe's moral superior by agreeing to keep as his own
the child that Joe has gotten on Tony's wife Amy. Motivated in part by his desire for an heir to his hard-earned
possessions, Tony acts primarily out of love for Amy and
sympathy for Joe.

Further suspicion is cast upon Joe's politics by Amy,
who despite her one indiscretion is a puritan at heart, constantly extolling the virtues of hard work and responsibility.
In her opinion, Joe's radicalism is his excuse for not getting down to business. "Wobbly" to her is just another
name for "hobo." Sarcastically, she tells him that it must
be nice to beat around the countryside, "no ties, work a
day, bum a week..." (300). At her parents' farm, she
says, they set the dog on the likes of Joe.

The play leaves the impression that in America, one
can, through hard work, without exploiting others and keeping one's humanity intact, get rich. Tony has money because he is virtuous; and, furthermore, he is virtuous be-

cause he has money. He uses his wealth to do good, and
while he would not want his money taken from him, he is
quick to give it away. They Knew What They Wanted seems
to say that a system which encourages the rise of a man
like Tony should be preserved, and that the motives of those
who would change it should be viewed with suspicion.

While few plays in this group approach the idealiza-
tion of the self-made man found in They Knew What They
Wanted, several give unqualified approval to the work ethic
detached from the pursuit of money. In these plays, the
protagonists reject the money definition of success. To
them, the summum bonum in life is not pecuniary reward;
instead, their lives are monuments to relentless work and
unremitting devotion to duty.

In the earliest of these plays, Why Marry ? by Jesse
Lynch Williams, [11] the recipient of the first Pulitzer Prize
for Drama in 1917, the heroine, Helen, is set apart from
the vapid, unproductive, and unhappy women of her class by
her competence as a scientist. Her colleague and fiance,
Dr. Ernest Hamilton, a brilliant medical researcher, is an
early example of that now familiar stereotype--the doctor
who works himself half to death for humanitarian rather than
mercenary motives. Foils to Helen and Ernest are Helen's
odious brother John, described by Williams as "the master-
ful type of successful American businessman" (27), and Lucy,
his parasitic wife.

The characters in this play provide a fairly comprehensive view of the American upper-middle class. John and
Rex Baker, a wealthy and well-connected young man John
hopes to marry off to his sister Jean, represent the capitalist class. John, in fact, is a captain of industry, but
Rex is the playboy-son of a rich father. That he is drunk

nearly every day indicates the dangers of idleness and in-
herited money (a theme constantly hammered out in the
bibles counseling young men in the get-ahead ethic). [12]   The
professions are represented by Uncle Theodore, a genteel
but poor clergyman; Uncle Everette, a judge who refers to
himself as a "jackal of Big Business" (47-48); and finally by Ernest, who has rejected a lucrative private practice in order to continue his dramatic but ill-paid research.

   While the play affirms the nobility of selfless dedication to duty, it also satirizes a society which does not reward those who make significant contributions.   Uncle Everette, the voice of the playwright, observes that in America,
one is rewarded in inverse proportion to his usefulness to
society.   He says, by way of example, that John and old man
Baker are rewarded most for "keeping up the cost of living."
For saving the constitution of a country which the Judge has
already admitted values private property over human life,
Uncle Everette gets the next largest share.   Then comes
the superintendent of John's mill, whose function is to cut
down on wages and operating costs so John can make a large
profit.   For saving human lives (often at the risk of his own),
Ernest gets a mere three thousand a year.   Finally, for
"saving immortal souls," Uncle Theodore gets next to nothing (41-42).   What the play says, finally, is that although
work does not necessarily add up to material rewards, it
should; and it argues that there is something grotesque about
a society in which such is not the case.

   Men in White, [13] Sidney Kingsley's 1933-34 Pulitzer
Prize winner and the prototype of the now ubiquitous soap
opera-medic show, goes considerably beyond Why Marry? in
glorifying the work ethic and condemning the get-rich morality.   Why Marry? suggested that good doctors should be re-

warded materially; <u>Men in White,</u> on the other hand, seems
to say that a doctor's life must be austere.

The play is a modern morality in which young George
Fergusson must choose, in Winifred Dusenbury's words, between "a life of economic, social, married happiness and one
of consecration to medicine."[14] The path to salvation is
illuminated by several characters in the play, chiefly by
George's mentor Dr. Hochberg, whose name suggests his
lofty ideals and whose example teaches the rejection of materialism in favor of unremitting toil and professional excel-
lence. George's father, too, was a selfless practitioner
who died of a heart attack because he could not bring himself to retire from the service of humanity.

Like Ernest in <u>Why Marry?</u> George is in love, but
his fiancee is no Helen. Laura, rich and spoiled, tempts
George to abandon the rigors of his life for an exclusive
private practice. Standing as she does for a life of leisure,
pleasure, and the pursuit of material goods, she is the test
George must pass in order to become a good doctor and a
good person as well.

If he fails to reject Laura and her values, he will,
Kingsley suggests, turn out like the materialists in the play,
all of whom are unsympathetically portrayed. One, Dr.
Cunningham, has a wealthy Park Avenue clientele and a reputation for incompetence among the internes and nurses.
Another is Laura's father, a caricature of the American
businessman. Like Dr. Hochberg, he works obsessively;
but he works solely for money and cannot understand why
George works so hard for so little return. Also presented
in a bad light are the businessmen who sit on the board of
the hospital. Their venal attitudes are as much a contrast
to the selfless dedication of Hochberg as the richly appointed
board room is to the austere quarters the doctors occupy.

When George, given an ultimatum by Laura that he
enter private practice so they can "live like human beings, "
rejects her to resume his study and research, he aligns
himself with all that is noble in his profession--grinding toil
and indifference to money.   That he has made the right
choice is confirmed by Hochberg, who tells him that devotion to healing rewards one with something richer than
money, "a kind of success that the world out there can't
measure ... a kind of glory... " (846).

Another play which denigrates the get-ahead gospel
and upholds the need for vocation is Eugene O'Neill's
Strange Interlude, [15] the Pulitzer Prize winner of 1928-29.
While the primary focus is upon the female protagonist,
Nina Leeds, three of the male characters, Sam Evans, Ned
Darrell, and Charles Marsden--businessman, scientist, and
artist--demonstrate the hollowness of the American Dream
and the need for a nobler ideal.

The embodiment of Horatio Alger aspirations in this
play is Sam Evans, who marries Nina, a girl on the verge
of collapse after the death of her fiance.   Nina's doctor and
friend, Ned Darrell, believing that a stable marriage will
save her, engineers the match, partly because Sam is kind
and affectionate, but also because he seems likely to "get
on" in the world.   Unfortunately, he turns out to be a slow
starter.   He wants desperately to "make good, " he works
hard, he studies success gospels like Mind Control for Success; but lacking confidence in himself because he thinks he
is sterile, he goes from job to job until news of Nina's
pregnancy restores his faith in himself.   It is no matter
that the child is fathered by Ned Darrell, now Nina's lover.
The effect is miraculous all the same.

Sam now dives into his work with renewed energy,

increases his earnings, and buys the advertising agency that
ultimately makes him a rich man.   Sam's material success
squares with the cherished American notion that a man,
properly motivated, with a little intelligence (and Sam appears to have very little), and a great deal of hard work,
can "succeed." The play insists, however, that Sam's as-
cent up the ladder of success is no victory for the human
spirit.   The price he pays is a coarsened nature and a loss
of the sensitivity which was his most engaging trait.   He
becomes a complacent and self-satisfied braggart, the arche-
typical American businessman, complete with obesity, high
blood pressure, and finally, a fatal stroke.

Although the play condemns striving after material
goods even when that drive is yoked to the family unit (Sam
only wants to "make good" for Nina and the baby), it strongly suggests the need for genuine vocation and upholds the
sanctity of work.   Ned Darrell, for example, is very nearly
destroyed because he gives up the thing that should have
been most important to him, his career as a doctor.
Blinded by love for Nina (who refuses to leave her husband),
Ned gives up his medical studies to be close to her.   His
character deteriorates from this point, and O'Neill describes
him as a man "with no definite aim or ambition to which he
can relate his living" (503).   Nina now finds him tedious but
accepts no guilt for his unhappiness: "No woman," she
says, "can make a man happy who has no purpose in life!"
(504).

Significantly, Ned's redemption comes through work.
After making a fortune by investing in Sam's business, Ned
takes up biology as a hobby.   Nina contemptuously dismisses
his new interest as "dabbling," and at first he does use his
laboratory, as he had once used women and drink, to blot

Nina from his mind. By the end of the play, however, science has reclaimed him, and he throws off his enslavement to a woman he could neither possess nor abandon.

Another foil for Sam is the Prufrockian character, Charles Marsden, whom Nina marries after Sam dies. A writer and a man of private means, Marsden has little sympathy for Sam's get-rich philosophy, and he utters the play's strongest anti-business sentiments. He thinks that Sam's kind are "inheriting the earth ... hogging it ... cramming it down their tasteless gullets" (490). Later, in a sweeping indictment of Sam and by extension of all American businessmen, he thinks, "What a fount of meaningless energy he's tapped!" To Marsden, the ceaseless movement demanded by the success-ethic obscures the fact that the end is not worth pursuing (495).

Marsden chides himself for taking this superior tone, however, because in his own terms, he, too, has failed. Like Ned, Marsden has betrayed his talent, turned his back on his real vocation as a writer. Instead of devoting himself to serious fiction, he dashes off genteel, superficial novels; but he has not sold out for money or popular success. The fact that he has both is incidental. His is finally a failure of nerve. He simply lacks the courage to face and "write the truth."

Of the three male characters, Marsden, who does not lust after fame or fortune, has the purest ideal. Ned, although money was never important to him, did yearn for fame and later laments giving up his chance to be "the world's greatest neurologist" (524). His dream of fame was, however, always mixed with humanitarian impulses and with a sense of calling he feels guilty for having denied. In the end, he is content to be "a worker in the ranks," and he tells Nina that through his work, he has "paid his debt" (519).

Finally, of course, Sam is the only man in the play who "succeeds," but his success seems less worthy than the failure of Ned and Marsden. O'Neill, who was fond of castigating American materialism, often made the businessman "the very devil's disciple, "[16] but Sam is nothing so grandiose. He is, in fact, a man of good will. O'Neill's tactic in Strange Interlude is to make the businessman naive and shallow, thus emphasizing the petty and adolescent quality of the American Dream and the emptiness of its achievement.

The Pulitzer Prize and Circle Award winner for 1939-40, William Saroyan's The Time of Your Life, [17] seems at first to reject both the success ethic and the work ethic as well, but ultimately it upholds them both with qualifications.

Saroyan's one-page preface to the play exhorts the reader to place "in matter and in flesh the least of the values, for these are the things that hold death and must pass away" (698). The play's central character, Joe, a young man John Gassner describes as having "acquired money and sickened of it, "[18] tries to live by this philosophy. Joe once worked hard, but quit in disgust when he realized that accumulating money hurt others. He now loafs in bars and spends as much as he can, but his money earns money. His income prevents him from living a "civilized life, " one which is harmful to no one, and he is glad he does not know anyone he may have hurt in his rise to wealth.

In addition to having rejected the success ethic, Joe appears to have rejected the work ethic as well. He explains that he drinks and loafs because if he does not, he becomes "fascinated by unimportant things. " He gets busy.

A life of doing things, of being busy, he equates with death, but by drinking and loafing, he says, "I live all the time" (680).

In spite of his effusions about the joys of leisure, he later reveals himself to be deeply troubled by his idleness. He tells a friend, "You can't enjoy living unless you work. Unless you do something." Unfortunately, Joe is too smart and lacks the patience to do "simple, good things," and other pursuits would just bring in more money. To Joe, all work is bound up in the success ethic except the least remunerative jobs, and these he is unsuited to do.

The necessity of doing "simple, good things" receives further emphasis when Joe gets his side-kick Tom a job driving a truck so he can marry his sweetheart Kitty Duval, a waterfront prostitute. Tom, who used to aspire to Joe's mode of life, responds with a lyrical outburst at the prospect of being a truck driver: "Travel. Highways. Little towns. Coffee and hot cakes. Beautiful valleys and mountains and streams and trees and daybreak and sunset." Joe says wistfully, "there is poetry in that" (694-695). Furthermore, the job will be the means for Tom to rescue Kitty from a life on the streets and to help her fulfill her dream, a dream expressed, incidentally, in material terms. What Kitty longs for is a big house with a big lawn, flower-beds and collie dogs all around.

What the play rejects, then, is not the necessity to work or the necessity to have some money in order to survive and be happy. The play, like Joe, is in reaction, as Howard R. Floan suggests, against "the vast impersonality of the new economics,"[19] a system in which rich people steal, as Joe expresses it, not "from rich people who can spare it, but from poor people who can't" (690). But in doing "simple, good things, " in making an honest living, there is "poetry" enough in that.

Two plays, both products of the Depression years, reject not only the success ethic but the work ethic as well. The earlier one, You Can't Take It With You, the George Kaufman-Moss Hart comedy which won the Pulitzer Prize for 1936-37, [20] is, in the words of one critic, a "jazzy restatement of the carpe diem theme, "[21] and according to another, is "characteristic of its time and genre in its brazen nose-thumbing at the world. "[22]

The play celebrates Grandpa Vanderhof and his eccentric family, people who "just don't care about the things other people give their lives to" (946). Impinged upon very little by the world outside, they "do their own thing"--hunt snakes, write plays, dance, play music, and make fireworks. Insanely busy having a good time, they are also an extremely happy and loving group because they have plenty of time for each other.

When the play juxtaposes Grandpa with Mr. Kirby (the father of a young man courting Vanderhof's granddaughter), Kirby, the typical American businessman--irrascible, convention-ridden, and plagued with indigestion--comes off a poor second. The confrontation allows Vanderhof to enlarge upon his philosophy. He explains that although he was once on his way to making a fortune, he quit business when he realized he was not having any fun. Now, he says, he is not obliged to work six hours at something he hates in order to earn one hour to spend as he likes.

At first, Kirby heartily disapproves and pronounces Grandpa's style of life dangerously un-American, even communistic (980), but by the end of the play, joie de vivre has won the day. Grandpa converts young Kirby outright, and

even Mr. Kirby appears to be reassessing his assumptions
about the efficacy of work.

In the Circle Award winner for the following year,
Maxwell Anderson's High Tor, [23] the protagonist, a Thoreau-
vian fellow named Van Van Dorn, shows much the same contempt for both work and money as Grandpa Vanderhof. Van
works three weeks a year as a mason in order to sustain
himself for the rest of the time. He once worked in an
automobile factory right across the river from Sing Sing
prison, but quit as soon as he realized that there was little
difference between the two institutions. He cannot understand why any man should labor forty years to earn time
off when he could be permanently on vacation by changing
his values.

Van's sweetheart, who has conventional notions about
work and financial security, threatens to leave him unless
he sells his part of High Tor, a mountain overlooking the
Hudson. Van refuses because he hates money, and he hates
progress, especially if it means digging out the mountain for
commercial purposes. In the end, he capitulates, not for
the money and not to placate the girl (who has already been
won over to his point of view), but because an old Indian
tells him that trying to stop progress is futile. Van decides
to sell and go west so that he and the girl can live undis-
turbed by the onslaught of modern civilization.

The play, although it denounces the dream of commercial success, does call up an earlier version of the
American Dream. As Gerald Rabkin observes: "The vision
which Van (and Anderson) champion belongs to the past, to
an agrarian society ... in which man has maximum freedom."[24] The play suggests that while modern America can
provide material success, the price--the natural beauty of

the land and the freedom of the individual--is too high, but
it also suggests that the tide of "material progress" is too
strong to be held back, even by the good, strong man.

The blanket rejection in these two plays of the work
ethic makes them atypical of prize-winning drama, which
usually assumes the need for some kind of job.   Many of the
plays, however, reject the success ethic just as strongly.
In fact, one of the pervasive themes in popular American
drama is the warping effect the American dream of success
has upon the human personality.   Many condemn materialism
by showing the ruined lives of those who live by the dream
but who are, in spite of their faith, unable to succeed in financial terms.

Perhaps the most celebrated American play treating
this theme is Arthur Miller's Death of a Salesman. [25]   The
protagonist of this play is Willy Loman, an aging salesman.
Unable to attain his absurdly false ideal of success, Willy
commits suicide in order to leave his insurance money to
his son Biff, so that Biff may go into business and succeed
where his father has failed.   At the end of the play, however, Biff rejects the dream in favor of that older American
dream, the vision of peace and freedom outside a competi-
tive society.

Like Van Van Dorn in High Tor and Grandpa Vanderhof in You Can't Take It With You, Biff hates business.   To
him, "it's a measly existence. " He tells his brother Hap
that it seems a sad thing to "suffer fifty weeks of the year
for the sake of a two-week vacation, when all you really desire is to be outdoors, with your shirt off" (1023).   Unfortunately for Biff, his father has so infected him with his
mad, get-ahead schemes, reinforced daily with maxims from
the success bibles, that Biff is thirty-four before he dis-

covers what he wants to do with his life. Hap, on the other
hand, has internalized Willy's philosophy, and even though
he is not content and knows that his father has never been
happy, he nonetheless intends to devote his life to the pursuit of success in business.

The conflict between Willy and Biff represents a clash
between two versions of the American dream--the urban business success goal and the rural-agrarian dream of the myth
of the garden. [26] The dream of business success, furthermore, is presented in Miller's play with variations. Willy's
Uncle Ben, for example, represents the ruthless, robber-
baron mentality, and Howard, Willy's boss, is an unsympa-
thetic version of the cold, impersonal materialist who puts
profits before human values. The pure Algerine belief that
an upright man can by honest work achieve success, however, is embodied in the play by Willy's neighbor Charley,
a successful businessman, and by his son Bernard, a respected lawyer. Charlie and Bernard live by what has been
termed the "character ethic, " while Willy adheres to the
"personality ethic, " the notion that one will succeed if one
is popular. [27] The play thus reflects that distortion in
America of the old Protestant ethic into the belief that per-
sonality-selling is the way to wealth. [28] Willy never considered honesty or hard work important; to him, being "well-
liked" was everything. He inculcates his sleazy standards
in his two boys by scoffing at the studious Bernard and by
encouraging his sons to steal, lie, and cheat their way
through life. They were not, as Biff observed, brought up
"to grub for money. " That they were good-looking and per-
sonable was, to Willy's way of thinking, enough to insure
success.

The relationship of this play to the American dream

of success has often been the subject of disagreement.
Some critics have branded it a Marxist tract; while others
say that Miller shied away from indicting the capitalist system strongly enough. [29] Some complain that Death of A
Salesman lacks a coherent viewpoint.   Another states bluntly
that Miller "does not understand his own play."[30] The confusion arises, it seems to me, from a failure to distinguish
between the "character ethic," which the play affirms, and
the "personality ethic," which it condemns.   Further difficulty arises if one assumes that Miller posits as best those
values finally embraced by Biff--nature, freedom, and the
simple life.   If such were the case, those critics who see
Bernard as a "norm of fulfillment" would be correct in as-
suming that the play is incoherent. [31]

What the play argues for primarily is the efficacy of
the Socratic dictum, "Know Thyself." Willy's tragedy is not
that he never made a lot of money, but that, as Biff per-
ceptively observes, "He never knew who he was" (1054).
The play suggests, then, that if a man wants to go into business, he can, like Charley ("the most decent man in the
play" by Miller's own assessment), [32] work hard and succeed in material terms and in human terms as well.   If,
however, he knows that he has little taste for bourgeois life,
he can pursue any course that interests him (being outdoors
with his shirt off, in the play's terms), so long as he understands that his worth has nothing to do with the amount of
money he earns. Willy, the play makes clear, liked to
work with his hands: "there's more of him in that front
stoop than in all the sales he ever made," according to Biff
(1054). Had he not been so perniciously infected with the
notion that success means earning money, he could have
made for himself a comely and satisfying life as a crafts-

man. His initial mistake was choosing an occupation for
which he was basically unsuited. He then compounded the
error by choosing the "personality ethic" instead of "the
character ethic." The play, it would seem, does affirm the
possibility of success and happiness in either version of the
American dream, commercial or noncommercial. What it
roundly condemns is the notion that merely making money,
whatever the cost in terms of honesty, integrity, or personal satisfaction, is success.

A more recent play which explores the frustration of
a man with the wrong standard of success is Who's Afraid
of Virginia Woolf? by Edward Albee, [33] a relentless critic
of the American dream and of the tone of American life in
general. This play is structured around the titanic quarrels
of George, a history professor, and his wife Martha, the
daughter of the college president. Witnesses to the carnage
who are later drawn into the fray themselves are Nick, a
young biologist new to the faculty, and his simpering wife
Honey.

According to this play, success in academia means
moving up through the ranks of the hierarchy to the top, not
by distinguishing oneself as a teacher or scholar, but by ag-
gressively jockeying for position and beating out the competi-
tion. In these terms, George has failed. He is, as Martha
gratuitously complains to the guests, "bogged down" in the
history department. His failure to advance is apparently not
due to laziness (he has written a book and some articles)
nor to lack of intelligence. He is simply not a go-getter
and is temperamentally unsuited to academic politics. Instead, he is of a contemplative turn of mind, a "bookworm,"
according to Martha; and she is probably right when she accuses him of lacking the "push," the "aggressiveness," and

the "personality, "--the "guts, " in short--to succeed (167).
The play suggests, in fact, that George would have an uneasy
stomach about resorting to some of the things required to
succeed in academic politics.   Martha, who worships her
father's success, finds this squeamishness absurd and suspects that the "high moral sense" which prevents George
from trying to "better himself" is merely an excuse (173).

Nick, on the other hand, is obviously a man on his
way up.   Although he is less intelligent than George, he is
anxious to find the levers of power.   Since he lacks George's
fastidiousness, he is quite willing to toady, to be a gigolo,
or to do whatever else seems indicated.   His plan is ruthlessly simple.   He has already married for money.   Now
he intends to "insinuate" himself into his department, make
himself an "inevitability, " gradually take over the duties of
his superiors, and, in order to consolidate his gains, "plow
a few pertinent wives" (173).

Oddly enough, although George rejects the means to
advancement, he accepts the goals of success.   Thus, he
becomes a failure in his own terms as well as in Martha's.
He accepts guilt for being "bogged down, " accepts Martha's
taunts about the size of their house and the amount of his
salary, accepts even her assessment of him as "a worm"
going nowhere except the grave (185).   Because he sees himself as a failure, Martha can induce instant maximum humil-
iation simply by calling him one.

Ironically, Martha, who accepts the success ethic as
practiced by her father, is contemptuous of Nick's way to
wealth.   After Nick attempts to make love to her, she says
scornfully, "You're ambitious, aren't you boy?" (191), and
accuses him of pursuing her in order to advance his career.
Furthermore, the qualities she admires in George--his

tolerance, his kindness, his goodness, in short--are the
very ones which prevent his use of tactics like Nick's.   One
critic has written that Martha's frustrations stem from the
"wrong choice of a man." What she needed, he says, was
a man who "vicariously would fulfill her desire to inherit
her father's power and position...."[34] Nick, it is true, has
the makings of such a man, but she scorns his machinations.
She freely confesses to Nick, in fact, that George is the
only man she loves, the only man who satisfies her.

As for George, he is, like Willy Loman, a failure on
two levels.   He falls short of success in terms of money
and prestige.   What is worse, he never realizes that having
succeeded he would probably have still been a failure.   Like
Death of a Salesman, the play implies that perhaps the dream
was not worth pursuing.

A recent prize-winning play which insists on the tawdriness of the American dream is John Guare's The House
of Blue Leaves.[35] The play, which takes place on the day
the Pope visited New York, concerns a frustrated zookeeper,
Artie Shaughnessy, who yearns to become a rich and famous
Hollywood songwriter.   Artie is a longtime resident of
Queens, a place that is symptomatic of his failure, for as
Guare points out in the introduction to the play, successful
people leave Queens for Scarsdale or Rye as soon as they
get the inevitable break, "the birthright of every American."
Artie, now "too old to be a young talent" (12), is still desperately singing his songs to unappreciative audiences on
amateur night at a bar significantly called El Dorado.

To add to his troubles, his wife, Bananas, is quite
mad, and his son Ronnie is another example of what happens to ordinary people in a country which promises fame
and fortune but seldom delivers.   Ronnie, whose life was

wrecked when he was not selected to play the lead in a
movie version of Huckleberry Finn, plans to blow up the
Pope with a homemade bomb in order to get the notoriety he
craves.

The one successful character in the play, Artie's old
friend Billy Einhorn, now a famous Hollywood moviemaker,
provides further comment on the American idea of "making
it." At the beginning of his career, Billy made a film that
subsequently became a classic and is still shown from time
to time at the Museum of Modern Art. Now, however, at
the height of his fame, he makes commercial movies with
Doris Day and Rock Hudson. No one in the play, least of
all Billy himself, seems to realize that he has sold out his
talent.

The play makes the shallowness of these feverish
characters obvious enough, but the Pope's visit is a brilliant
ironic device which drives the point home. Shortly after the
Pope's procession through Queens, three celebrity-mad nuns
invite themselves into Artie's apartment, hoping to catch a
glimpse of Jackie Kennedy or Cardinal Spellman on television,
a comment on the commercial quality of American Catholicism. Later that night, when the Pope's image appears on
the screen, he makes a speech commending the American
people for basing their conception of life "on spiritual values, "
and for safeguarding the American spirit from the dangers of
materialism (79-80).

These three plays all expose the folly of pursuing material success by showing the misery of people who do not
realize their dreams. Another group of prize-winning plays
attacks the American dream from a different vantage point
by showing the unhappiness of those who do.

An early play which unambiguously condemns devotion

to crass materialism by showing the corruption of one who succeeds is Eugene O'Neill's <u>Beyond the Horizon</u> (1919-20). [36]   O'Neill, it should be noted, always "vigorously rejects the success-ethic, " according to Frederic I. Carpenter, and condemns the American dream as nothing more than "the dream of material things. "[37]   A constant thread in his plays, however, from <u>Beyond the Horizon</u> to <u>Long Day's Journey Into Night</u>, is that one can achieve material success if he is willing to sacrifice his soul in the process.

<u>Beyond the Horizon</u> juxtaposes two brothers, Robert, a dreamy idealist who cares little for practical considerations, and Andrew, who always has his eye on the main chance.   O'Neill, as he would do later in <u>Strange Interlude,</u> makes the commercial type a decent fellow but something of a clod.   Andrew has no insight into his brother's values, regards education as useless, and poetry as silly: "Imagine me reading poetry and plowing at the same time!   The team'd run away..." (60).   Andrew is a farmer to the core, but the drive to make money is already strong in him.   He aims, he says, to make the family farm into "one of the slickest, best paying" ones in the state (67).   When he learns that Robert wants to go to sea, he assumes that he wants to study navigation and become an officer because "there's fair pay in it..." (61).   Utterly incapable of understanding that Robert's longing to go to sea is a way of following his dream of beauty "beyond the horizon, " Andrew rambles on about the many opportunities waiting for "a fellow with his eyes open" and assumes that Robert (like Willy Loman's brother Ben) will come back a millionaire.

Robert's plans go awry when Andrew's sweetheart confesses her love for Robert rather than Andrew.   Robert marries and stays on the farm, while Andrew ships out in

his place.   Predictably, Robert fails as a farmer, and because material success is so often equated with masculinity
in American culture, Ruth taunts him by saying that Andrew
is "twice the man" that he is and tells him, furthermore,
that she hates being married to one who is not "man enough"
to make money (83).   The identification of success with
masculinity is, incidentally, a common thread in these plays,
clearly visible, for example, in Who's Afraid of Virginia
Woolf?, Raisin in the Sun, and Strange Interlude.

        Meanwhile, Andrew, now the hope of the family, has
grown rich.   Ironically, the voyage which would have saved
Robert has ruined Andrew, for as soon as he saw the Ar-
gentine, he gave himself over to the pursuit of money.   His
reaction is the straight Alger cliche: "I'm going to make
good right from the minute I land, if working hard and a determination to get on can do it and I know they can!" (88).
He does amass a fortune, but he also acquires a look of
"ruthless cunning" and an avaricious streak which causes
him to lose everything in speculation.   What is worse, Andrew, like Willy Loman, does not know who he is.   He has,
as Robert points out, spent eight years running from himself (100).

        The parade of characters in popular American drama
who are, like Andrew, corrupted by the pursuit of riches,
who become dishonest, rapacious, or stingy, who are less
somehow than they could be, is a long one.   For example,
Joe Keller in Arthur Miller's All My Sons is a man who
justifies the shadiest business practices in his determination
to build up the family business.   James Tyrone, the pom-
pous, miserly actor in Eugene O'Neill's Long Day's Journey
Into Night is a man who threw away his talent as an actor
in favor of money, who always makes economies in all the

wrong places.   John Cleary, the father in The Subject Was
Roses is another miser.

Similarly afflicted is Eliza, the penny-mad mother in
Ketti Frings' dramatization of the Thomas Wolfe novel, Look
Homeward, Angel. [38]   Eliza is consumed with the need to
work tirelessly, to turn a profit, to save bottles and string,
to spout the Alger cliches at her children.   A foil for Eliza
is her husband, Oliver Gant, a wild, Rabelaisian romantic,
a sculptor debased into a stonecutter, but who is nevertheless above the petty world of buying, saving, and selling.
According to one critic, Eliza is "the symbol of American
materialsim, " while Gant is "the opposing symbol of the
ideal of freedom. "[39]   Eliza is not treated without sympathy
in the play, but her compulsively materialistic orientation is
made to appear unwholesome.   Her values, for example, are
equated with those of the local whoremistress.   The madame
tells Gant that she and Eliza are alike because each of them
understands that property is what makes a person hold his
head up (261).

The spiritual dislocations which accompany the worship of Mammon receive heavy stress in two prize-winning
plays dealing with black people, Lorraine Hansberry's A
Raisin in the Sun[40] and Charles Gordone's No Place To Be
Somebody. [41]   For the black man, so long denied equal opportunity in this country, the American dream has been for
the most part the white man's dream.   Both of these plays
suggest, however, that the feverish pursuit of money is also
the white man's disease, which Negroes would do well to
eschew.

In A Raisin in the Sun, for example, Lena Younger,
the wise old matriarch, knows that her family needs larger
and cleaner quarters, just as her scrawny pot plant needs

sunshine and fresh air. Her daughter Beneatha needs an expensive education in order to become a doctor, and her son
Walter Lee needs more money because his wife Ruth is expecting another child. Fortunately, Lena is due to receive
ten thousand dollars, her late husband's insurance money.
The complication arises, however, when Walter Lee, severely afflicted with the need to get rich, wants to use the money
to invest in a liquor store.

Lena is basically anti-business. She says that too
much talk about money "ain't Christian, " and keeps reminding Walter that they are not business people but "just plain
working people" (29-30). To Lena, money is only important
because it will provide her family with a decent standard of
living and a small measure of security. Her values are
firmly centered upon the family unit.

To Walter Lee, on the other hand, money "is life"
(61). He wants more than mere comfort. He needs to be
rich, to be respected, to have power. He dreams of having
an office downtown, of bossing underlings, of driving a
Chrysler, of having a large house and a spacious lawn with
a gardener in attendance, of sending his son to a prestigious
university. He finds Lena's limited wants absurd and believes that Negroes have failed to advance because they are
"tied to a race of women with small minds" (23).

Finally, Lena uses part of the money as a down pay-
ment on a house. The rest she turns over to Walter Lee
because she senses that her position as head of the household has undermined his masculinity. He is promptly
swindled, but he finally comes into his manhood when he rejects the offer of a citizen's group which wants to pay the
Youngers not to move into their all-white neighborhood.
Walter has learned Lena's lesson at last: one does not put
money before pride or the integrity of the family. [42]

Like <u>A Raisin in the Sun,</u> <u>No Place To Be Somebody</u>
provides an answer to Langston Hughes' question, "What happens to a dream deferred?" At least two characters in this
play have come to realize that the American dream, especially for the black man, is a chimera. Gabe, a poet and an
actor, says that his college education did not give him "that
introduction to success, equality an' wealth" that to his
parents were "the most logical introduction to heaven" (21).
Gabe's gentle irony provides a contrast to the corrosive
bitterness of Johnny, a black saloon-owner. He speaks
scornfully of the American dream: "Still think you kin sell
papers an' become president, huh? Snowballs in Egypt"
(18). His disillusionment has bred in him a contempt for
the system. He assumes, for example, that since the rewards of the system are not generally available to the black
man, he is under no compulsion to obey the laws of that
system.

Like Walter Lee, Johnny is obsessed with making
money, an affliction labeled in this play "Charley fever. "
According to Sweets Crane, the surrogate father who infected him with the fever and taught him to be a crook, getting Johnny an education or teaching him to "dinner pail"
would not guarantee that he would grow up to be "respected
like a man" (39). Only money confers that respect and presumably, the only way a black man can make a great deal
of it is through crime. Although Johnny has evidently
learned his lesson well, he is frustrated because his career
is limited to pimping and petty thievery, significant crime
in his district being the exclusive preserve of the Mafia.
Johnny has been counting on Sweets to help him break into
the rackets, but Sweets, now old and ill, has reformed.
He tells Johnny that "Charley fever" is a sickness. He in-

sists that the black man should not ape the worst character-
istics of the white man, and he tries to convince Johnny
that fine clothes and big cars do not make one a man (39).
Unlike Walter Lee, however, Johnny is incapable of redemption.   Presumably the disease has progressed too far, and
Johnny's greed and anger have twisted him beyond all hope
of repair.

Perhaps the saddest comments on the futility of
money-mongering are contained in those plays which show a
person who has reached the pinnacle only to find the victory
hollow.   Big Daddy Pollitt in Tennessee Williams' Cat on a
Hot Tin Roof, [43] a play which, in the words of one critic,
shows "the corrosive effects of the materialistic 'ethic' in
the rural south, "[44] is such a character.   Big Daddy quit
school at ten, began as an overseer, "worked like a nigger
in the fields, " and finally became a millionaire and the
owner of twenty-eight thousand acres of "the richest land
this side of the valley Nile" (65).   All of his life, he says,
he has been "like a doubled up fist ... poundin', smashin',
drivin'!" (969).   Big Daddy comes to realize, after it is too
late, that the money he worshipped has not brought him
pleasure or even respectability.   A man, he tells his son
Brick, can't use money "to buy back his life ... when his
life has been spent" (65).   His fortune is of no further use
to him, and will only be a legacy of hate over which his
disagreeable family will fight for years to come.

The American dream has been continuously subjected
to scrutiny in the most popular American drama, and many
plays--from Why Marry? to That Championship Season--have
cast doubts upon its worth.   Some have stridently proclaimed
the dream a cheat; others, like How to Succeed in Business
Without Really Trying, have tartly satirized it; many have

exposed it as an empty ideal, not worth its price in morality or integrity. Seldom do prize-winning plays glamorize zeal for wealth; a few will not even concede the efficacy of work.

Because so many of these plays assume that a life printed on dollar bills is no life at all, an observation Charles Kaplan makes in his discussion of You Can't Take It With You would seem to apply to popular American plays in general. They express, he says, "the irrepressible American idealism that constantly lurks just below the surface of our brazen materialism."[45] One might be tempted to cónclude that the American civilization, which these plays supposedly mirror, is not so money-hungry as we had been led to believe. What qualifies this conclusion, however, is the continuation of the complaints against the "success" disease.

NOTES

1. The Epic of America (Boston: Little, Brown, and Co., 1931), p. viii.

2. Frederic I. Carpenter, American Literature and the Dream (New York: Philosophical Library, Inc., 1955), p. 3.

3. Ibid., p. 5.

4. For a discussion of this fundamental idea and the attack recently mounted against it, see "Do Schools Make a Difference?" by Godfrey Hodgson, Atlantic Monthly (March, 1973), pp. 35-46.

5. According to Carpenter (p. 3), the "constant and omnipresent influence of the American dream" upon American literature accounts for the difference between American literature and the literature of England.

6. Irvin G. Wyllie in The Self-Made Man in America:

The Myth of Rags to Riches (New Brunswick, N. J.:
The Rutgers Univ. Press, 1954), p. 174, notes that
while scholars have piled up mountains of data prov-
ing that the self-made man in America is the exception and not the rule, men continue to believe because
the average man needs his dreams.

7. Wyllie (p. 138), asserts, for example, that in the nine-
teenth century, men of literary culture rarely tried
to conceal their contempt for the success ethic.
John Cawelti in Apostles of the Self-Made Man:
Changing Concepts of Success in America (Chicago:
The University of Chicago Press, 1965), p. 227,
says: "The central emphasis in twentieth-century
American fiction is on the woes of success."

8. Kenneth S. Lynn, The Dream of Success: A Study of
the Modern American Imagination (Boston: Little,
Brown and Co., 1955), p. 253.

9. The Pulitzer Prize Novels: A Critical Backward Look
(Norman: The University of Oklahoma Press, 1966),
p. 215.

10. A New Edition of the Pulitzer Prize Plays, ed. Kathryn Coe and William Cordell (New York: Random
House, 1940), pp. 275-316.

11. (New York: Charles Scribner's Sons, 1914.)

12. B. C. Forbes, for example, never tired of pouring
scorn and pity upon the "pampered sons of plutocrats"
who are handicapped in the world of affairs by having
had the misfortune to be born with a golden spoon in
their mouths. Quoted in Richard M. Huber, The
American Idea of Success (New York: McGraw-Hill
Book Co., 1971), p. 215.

13. A New Edition of the Pulitzer Prize Plays, pp. 794-
847.

14. The Theme of Loneliness in Modern American Drama
(Gainesville: The University of Florida Press, 1960),
p. 186.

15. A New Edition of the Pulitzer Prize Plays, pp. 427-
539.

16. Frederic I. Carpenter, Eugene O'Neill (New York:
     Twayne Publishers, Inc., 1964), p. 69.

17. Masters of Modern Drama, ed. Haskell M. Block and
     Robert G. Shedd (New York: Random House, 1962),
     pp. 671-698.

18. Dramatic Soundings (New York: Crown Publishers,
     1968), p. 409.

19. William Saroyan (New York: Twayne Publishers, Inc.,
     1966), p. 102.

20. A New Edition of the Pulitzer Prize Plays, pp. 923-
     983.

21. Charles Kaplan, "Two Depression Plays and Broadway's
     Popular Idealism, " American Quarterly, XV (1963),
     583.

22. Edmond M. Gagey, Revolution in American Drama
     (New York: Columbia University Press, 1947),
     p. 230.

23. (Washington, D.C.: Anderson House, 1937.)

24. Drama of Commitment: Politics in the American
     Theatre of the Thirties (Bloomington: The Indiana
     University Press, 1964), pp. 284-285.

25. Masters of Modern Drama, pp. 1020-1045.

26. Charles E. Eisinger, "Focus on Arthur Miller's Death
     of a Salesman: The Wrong Dreams, " American
     Dreams, American Nightmares, ed. David Madden
     (Carbondale: Southern Illinois University Press,
     1970), p. 165.

27. These terms are used by Richard M. Huber in his
     analysis (cited above) of the American ideal of suc-
     cess.

28. Lynn, p. 253.

29. For the playwright's discussion of and reaction to these
     divergent opinions, see his introduction to Arthur
     Miller's Collected Plays (New York: The Viking

Press, 1957), pp. 27-28.

30. John V. Hagopian, "Arthur Miller: The Salesman's Two Cases," Modern Drama, VI (1963-64), 124.

31. Richard J. Foster, in his article "Confusion and Tragedy: The Failure of Miller's Salesman," Two Modern American Tragedies, ed. James D. Hurrell (New York: Charles Scribner's Sons, 1961), 85-86, makes this complaint. He writes that "the bourgeois religion of success pretty well defeats the values that all along Miller had seemingly wished to pit against it."

32. Collected Plays, p. 37.

33. Best American Plays, Fifth Series, 1957-1963, ed. John Gassner (New York: Crown Publishers, Inc., 1963), pp. 143-201.

34. Harold Lamport made these observations in a Saturday Review article (June 29, 1963). The article is reproduced in Best American Plays, pp. 146-148.

35. (New York: The Viking Press, 1972.)

36. A New Edition of the Pulitzer Prize Plays, pp. 55-104.

37. "Focus on Eugene O'Neill's The Iceman Cometh," American Dreams, American Nightmares, p. 159.

38. (New York: Charles Scribner's Sons, 1958.)

39. Frederic I. Carpenter, American Literature and the Dream, p. 159.

40. (New York: The New American Library, 1958.)

41. (New York: The Bobbs-Merrill, Co., Inc., 1969.)

42. It is ironic, however, as C. W. E. Bigsby observes in Confrontation and Commitment (University of Missouri Press, 1967), p. 159, that the Youngers' spiritual regeneration is contingent upon the ten thousand dollars. Bigsby states that in making the money the "necessary prerequisite for their return to dignity and pride Hansberry would seem to demean the faith

in human potential which she is ostensibly endorsing. "

43. (New York: The New American Library, 1955.)

44. Esther Merle Jackson, The Broken World of Tennessee
     Williams (Madison: The University of Wisconsin
     Press, 1965), p. 134.

45. p. 585.

Chapter 3

WAR AND PHYSICAL VIOLENCE

To say that America is a violent society is by now, unfortunately, a commonplace. In this nation--conceived in rebellion, born in blood, expanded by ruthless aggression, consolidated in a savage civil struggle, and launched as an international power by participation in two world wars--violence is the order of the day. Assassination and attempted assassination have become almost a routine part of the political process; riot a familiar feature of the social scene; urban life a daily confrontation between aggressor and victim; rural America, in spite of a persistent tendency to romanticize it, sordid and as brutal as it always was.[1] Although some would prefer to view our conflicts, particularly those of the virulent Sixties as aberrations of American history, many thoughtful observers claim that the clashes of recent times were just business as usual, "the type of behavior often displayed in this country when there is a large division of purpose...," according to a recent commission report.[2] Many are now, in fact, forced to agree with Rap Brown: "Violence is as American as cherry pie."[3]

Because violence is such a conspicuous staple of American life, many of our most popular plays either address themselves to the problem or deal with it tangentially. As one would expect of a popular art growing out of a brutal

society, a good many of these plays reveal a tolerance for
violent behavior. A few, in fact, glorify it unabashedly,
and, while several make at least a perfunctory condemna-
tion, only two or three take an unequivocal stand against it.

The underlying assumption of many of the most respected American plays--those which won major drama
awards since 1917--is that violence is a fundamental part
of the human personality and therefore of human activity.
Such a position, according to one psychiatrist, [4] perpetuates
violence by accepting it as a donné of the life process, rather than the result of social conditioning. If this is so,
then some of the most popular American plays, even those
which seem on the surface to deplore violence, actually promote a tolerance for brutality by presenting it as an in-
eradicable fact of life.

Marc Connelly's The Green Pastures, [5] the Pulitzer
Prize winner for 1929-30, a play which many consider one
of the loveliest in American dramatic literature, is an example of a play which supports violence for a worthy purpose. In fact, in spite of the violence (or perhaps because
of it) some critics view the play as something of a religious
expression, a play which will make people better, the "divine comedy" of the modern theatre. [6] The play, which
recreates scenes from Old Testament history as Connelly
thought Southern Blacks understood it, is structured around
the struggles between De Lawd and the unruly race of men
he has created. While he worries about their laziness,
their gambling, drinking, and sexual promiscuity, it is their
tendency toward casual brutality and their indifference to the
suffering they inflict that mark how low they can sink.

The play suggests that the acceptance of violence is
dyed deep in the threads of human life, and given the char-

acter of the Creator, how could it be otherwise? God is depicted in The Green Pastures (as indeed he is in the Old Testament) as a God of wrath and vengeance. The violent strain in his character is not immediately apparent in the play, however, for the opening scenes take place in heaven. Here the angels are obedient and deferential, allowing De Lawd to play the majestic but benign parent.

With the creation of man De Lawd's troubles begin, and another side of Connelly's God is revealed--that of the frustrated father who tries to threaten his recalcitrant children into acceptable behavior but who finally resorts, out of sheer frustration, to furious retributions. Some indication of this facet of his character is given in his first reaction to man gone astray--the scene with Cain following the murder of Abel. De Lawd receives the news rather calmly, and although he does call the killing a crime, he never condemns violence outright. In fact, when Cain says that he would "bust anybody what make me de fool, " God replies, "Well, I ain't sayin' you right an' I ain't saying you wrong" (614).

Once he realizes that Cain is not unique, that mankind is evidently incorrigibly wicked, De Lawd begins to make such baleful statements as: "I got a good min' to wipe 'em all off an' people the earth with angels" (620). Later, he declares: "I am a god of wrath and vengeance an' dat's why I'm gonter destroy dis' worl' " (622). At this point, he begins his series of reprisals, letting them "feel de wrath" by causing the Flood, by hurling thunderbolts (a practice he abandons only because it is ineffectual), and by letting the Hebrews fall into bondage in Egypt. His ire also descends upon the Egyptians after their repeated acts of cruelty to the Hebrews. Later, when the Babylonians casu-

ally slay the prophet of the Lord, the dying man calls out:
"Smite 'em down, Lord, like you said. Dey ain't a decent
person left in de whole world" (642). God, now tired of
punishing, abandons mankind altogether. Up to this point in
the play, however, the pattern of his relationship with his
creatures has been one of violence countered by violence.

Significantly, De Lawd's final reconciliation with man
is achieved through violence and suffering. Rather unwilling-
ly, he is drawn back into the arena of human affairs when
it comes to his attention, through the prayers of Hezdrel, a
Hebrew soldier, that the Children of Israel are "fightin'
bravely" in the face of terrible odds against the invaders of
Jerusalem. De Lawd is as proud of Hezdrel's staunch defense of the Holy City as he is puzzled by his belief that
death will mean union with him: "We leap out of our skins, "
Hezdrel tells his followers, "right into de lap of God" (645).

Hezdrel, having abandoned faith in the "ol' God of
wrath and vengeance, " now worships the God of Hosea, a
god of mercy. De Lawd is clearly mystified, since mercy
is a side of his character that he does not, as yet, know
anything about. Hezdrel, now the Lawd's moral superior, [7]
explains that one learns mercy through suffering. De Lawd
then comes to realize that he, too, must suffer through the
death of Christ. In The Green Pastures, then, God is portrayed as a violent deity, and the men created in his image
are much given to savagery. In addition to suggesting that
ferocity is radical, the play glorifies a warrior for his determination to fight to the last man, whose heroism is revealed through the warcry: "Give 'em eve'ything, Boys!"
(647). The play shows war as a purifying agent, and violence and murder--specifically the crucifixion--as the means
through which mercy and reconciliation are obtained.

Another play which strongly indicates that violence is
basic to the human animal is Maxwell Anderson's Winterset, [8]
winner of the first Drama Critics' Circle Award in 1935-36.
The play, suggested by the Sacco-Vanzetti case of the early
twenties, centers around Mio Romagna, the son of a con-
fessed anarchist executed for a murder actually committed
by Trock Estrella, a gangster.   Mio, "half mad with hate"
(48), lives only to vindicate his father and to avenge his
death.   By the time he obtains certain knowledge of his
father's innocence, however, Mio has fallen in love with
Miriamne, the sister of a man who by his silence let Romagna die for Estrella's crime.   Mio's love for Miriamne
leads him to give up his thirst for vengeance, but too late.
The lovers are murdered in the street by Estrella's hench-
men.

The world of Winterset--a world where the poor are
oppressed, where the police are corrupt and brutal, where
"justice" is available only to the rich--is bleak indeed.   The
play says, moreover, that the problem lies beyond any one
political system or any one time.   It is the condition of
man.   This sombre view is reinforced in the play in part
through the imagery.   The many images of darkness, of ani-
mals--particularly small and vicious ones--and of physical
torture function, as Jacob Adler points out, to make the
world of Winterset as grim as that of King Lear.   Furthermore, what is suggested in the images is made explicit in
the speeches of two of the characters, Rabbi Esdras, Miriamne's father, and Judge Gaunt, who presided over the Romagna trial and who is now half crazed by the fear that he
sent an innocent man to his death.   Both men are old and
rich in experience; and both are convinced of man's inherent bestiality.

To Rabbi Esdras, life is grounded in violence:
"There's not one title to land or life, even your own, but
was built on rape and murder, " he tells Mio (71). Just as
he sees violence as a part of the life process, he believes
injustice is a fact of existence. The very ground we walk
on, he says, "is impacted down and hard with blood and
bones of those who died unjustly" (70-71).

The old Rabbi's Talmudic fatalism gives him at least
a kind of composure. Judge Gaunt, on the other hand, is
being driven mad over the conflict in his mind regarding violence and injustice. He abhors the use of violence and feels
guilty that the law he represents is based upon it. His
speeches in Act I to a policeman make amply clear that he
is haunted by nightmares rising from his bad conscience.
He warns the policeman that if a man must die "for the good
of many, " he should not make himself the "instrument of
death. " The brain, he says, "that delicate ganglion, will
not bear such things" (41).

The judge, in spite of his distaste for violence, believes in the inherent depravity of man, a philosophy which
justifies, even insists upon, the use of force on the grounds
that without it, man would immediately revert to savagery.
In his attempt to defend the concept of capital punishment,
he tells Mio: "Certain laws seem cruel in their operation;
it's necessary that we be cruel to uphold them. This
cruelty is kindness to those I serve" (73). He sees the law
as a dike holding back "anarchy and chaos. " Without law,
he declares, "men are beasts..." (75).

In the bleak world of Winterset, the best hope one
can have is to get out, the earlier the better. The judge,
for example, believes that life is an inevitable progress
from innocence to depravity. Only the young love truth and

justice. The old, he says, are "savage, wary, violent..."
(93). Esdras, too, in his speech over the bodies of Mio
and Miriamne, says that dying young is better than living to
a nihilistic old age. In such a world, the love of Mio and
Miriamne, like that of Romeo and Juliet, was bound to be
snuffed out, but in a world so evil, as Adler observes, one
is "better off for having left it."[10]

In contrast to The Green Pastures and Winterset,
Paul T. Nolan's prize-winning play, There's Death for the
Lonely,[11] dramatizes the belief that violence is not inevitable, but rather that it grows out of a sense of powerlessness and alienation--social conditions capable of amelioration.
According to the Introduction, Nolan conceived the idea for
the play during a period of shock and outrage following the
murder of President Kennedy. The play does not treat the
Kennedy assassination at all, but it does suggest that conditions favorable for violence are fostered by isolation and
despair. Death for the Lonely is a melodrama in the manner of the gangster movies of the thirties. It features a
sinister host, a la Vincent Price, who herds together a
group of people he forces to play a deadly game, one requiring that the guests vote for the loneliest among them.
The one selected wins the prize--death.

The guests represent the fringes of normal life--a
runaway housewife, a lesbian career woman, a displaced
Southerner, a lonely intellectual bachelor, a drifter, an alcoholic spinster, a young black girl. None is happy with
his life; none has any permanent or meaningful connections
with anyone else. The host is himself a cripple. The play
seems to suggest that loneliness and alienation foster a mel-
odramatic view of the world, an interpretation of life which
prompts one to see the world as made up of villains and

victims.   The alienated person, having written his own
script, then plays out the fatal drama in which he either
victimizes or is himself a victim.

Although these three plays are shaped of American
materials, all three transcend the particular social milieu of
the setting.   All ultimately ask fundamental questions about
the nature of man.   Several plays in this group, however,
deal more specifically with the problem of violence in America.   Robert Lowell's The Old Glory, [12] the Obie winner for
1964-65, suggests that current upheavals may be the result
of the peculiarly American character, a character which,
according to Robert Brustein, Lowell shows to be permeated
with violence from its beginnings--"a violence which invariably erupts out in moments of panic. "[13]

The first part of The Old Glory, a trilogy of one-act
plays, is My Kinsman, Major Molineaux.   Like the Haw-
thorne story on which it is based, My Kinsman shows the
American Revolution--enshrined though it is in our mythol-
ogy--as a particularly gruesome and nightmarish affair.
The play is set in Boston--"the city of the dead"--on the
eve of the Tea Party, and it shows, as Harold Clurman has
noted, the activists on both sides as "pimps, prostitutes,
fairies, hypocrites, turncoats--all more or less covered
with slime or gore, sometimes both. "[14]   The play insists
upon the point that schoolbooks often gloss over: that the
"meanest and most squalid sort of violence was ... put to
the service of Revolutionary ideals and objectives. "[15]

The second of these plays, [16] Benito Cereno, based
on the novella by Melville, addresses itself to that most pervasive of American problems--race relations.   Like My
Kinsman, Major Molineux, it suggests that the roots and
runners of present discord go deep into the American soil.

Set in 1800 off the coast of Trinidad, the play centers around
the encounter of two ships, The President Adams, an American merchant vessel, and The San Domingo, a ship carrying
a large cargo of slaves.   Amasa Delano, the American captain, boards the slave ship, which appears to be in trouble.
He hears from the blacks a tale of horrors: scurvy, yellow
fever, storms, famine, and thirst have plagued their cross-
ing.   Don Benito, the elegant young captain, is constantly
attended by an obsequious little Negro named Babu and seems
so dazed by hardship that he takes little interest in running
the ship.

        Captain Delano, slow though he is to catch on, finally
realizes that the slaves, led by Babu, control the ship, having made Don Benito their prisoner.   Just as the blacks demand that Captain Delano sail them back to Africa, men
from The President Adams board the ship and open fire on
the slaves.   When Babu cries that the future lies with the
black man, Delano shouts "This is your future," and empties
his pistol into the body of the black man.

        The action of the play, which shows Americans, mo-
tivated ostensibly by goodwill, entering a situation they do
not understand, misreading all the signs, and then siding
with the oppressors to slaughter the insurgents, parallels
our intervention in Vietnam, at least as critics of our
foreign policy see it.   The main point of the play, however,
is to reveal the kind of character which makes such an action possible.   If the two New Englanders, Captain Delano
and his bosun, John Perkins, are at all representative, the
American character is exposed as naive, jingoistic, anti-
intellectual, white supremist, and--growing out of these
flaws--extremely violent as well.

        The thoroughgoing bigotry of the two Americans, their

shameless assumption that "white is right, " is perhaps their
most characteristic trait.   Perkins, for example, in discussing the state of affairs on The San Domingo, concludes that
"Brown men in charge of black men" does not add up to
much (134).   Delano reveals a particularly ambivalent attitude about slavery.   He is frankly intrigued by the idea of
servitude.   He freely admits to Don Benito that Americans
sometimes "overdo our talk of freedom. "   In our hearts, he
confides, "we all want slaves" (177).   He comments further
that the Negro makes a particularly nice body servant:
something about him, Delano says, "makes him fit to have
around your person" (167).   Predictably, he mouths the
white supremist cliche that the admixture of Caucasian blood
benefits the darker races: "If we're so proud of our white
blood, surely a little added to the blacks improves their
breed" (175).

　　　　Incredibly, Captain Delano, who believes himself an
honorable and upright man, has no real sense of danger.
He senses that things are not as they should be on the slave
ship, but he asks repeatedly, "Who would want to kill Amasa
Delano?"   That the people whose humanity he so openly
qualifies might want to kill him is beyond his comprehension.
The ending of the play, in which Delano has the blacks mer-
cilessly cut down, follows logically from his insensitivity
and prejudice.   Thus, the play, according to one critic,
works "both a reminder of the violence of the American
heritage, and a warning of the possible violence in the American future. "[17]

　　　　That violence in the American heritage did indeed result in racial discord is amply demonstrated in nearly all
prize-winning plays which deal with blacks.   The plays, ac-
curately reflecting the climate of a country which has sys-

tematically and energetically excluded blacks from its mainstream, show violence as the means the white man uses to
keep the Negro "in his place." They also show that violent
behavior is the black man's response to his humiliating sense
of powerlessness. In a country which considers him something less than a person, violence is often his only means
of forging identity.

Paul Green's play of the twenties, In Abraham's
Bosom, [18] winner of the Pulitzer Prize in 1926-27, is a bitter
play about violence and its relationship to the black experience in America. The central character, Abraham McCranie,
is a mulatto, the illegitimate son of a rich planter. Abe
has evidently worked hard and kept his mouth shut (the
standard way of getting along with whites) until two years
before the play opens. At that time, the lynching of a young
black galvanized his resentment, and he began educating himself in the hope of becoming a leader of blacks. The other
Negroes on the plantation either fear or resent Abe's ambition. Most assume the basic inferiority of blacks, disapprove
of education and aspiration, and expect Abe's "uppity" atti-
tudes--which they attribute to his mixed blood--to get him
into trouble. Inevitably, they do. In fact, his career is one
long series of defeats, and physical as well as psychological
brutality is a fact of his life. Early in the play, for example, he is savagely beaten by his father, and toward the
end, he is attacked by whites who resent his preaching equality for blacks.

Abe, however, is no passive victim, but is himself a
man of violence. His murderous anger, always simmering
just below the surface, erupts many times during the play,
always with disastrous consequences. The beating he received from his father, was in fact, occasioned by Abe's

striking his half-brother Lonnie. Later, Abe is dismissed
from his position as a teacher after he punished an idle
child too severely. At the end of the play, Abe kills Lonnie,
an act which results in his own death at the hands of a white
lynch mob.

Clearly, however, his violence is a reaction to the
violence dealt him. He says of whites: "Dey stomp on me,
squash me, mash me in the ground like a worm" (418). Usually, Abe's anger is the result of immediate frustration;
sometimes, however, he vents his desire for general revenge. When he kills Lonnie, for example, he says: "Now
I'm going to pay somebody back. Now I'm going to get
even" (419). Even after Lonnie is dead, Abe continues to
beat him until "all the madness" is out. In addition to Abe's
frustration at being constantly thwarted and brutalized by the
white man, Abe also uses aggression to establish his identity. In a way, those characters who attribute his bitterness
to his mixed blood are right, for Abe is neither white nor
black, an illegitimate son, but yet casually acknowledged by
his father. He says of himself at one point, "I dunno what
I am" (417).

The abiding impression left by In Abraham's Bosom
is one of tragic loss. Due to the destructive effects of prejudice and violence, the energies and talents of an exceptional man are lost to the world. Two recent plays, both
by black playwrights, present a more complex picture of
black-white relations. While recognizing that violence on
both sides is the American way, neither play finally deplores
the situation as firmly as Green does.

LeRoi Jones, author of Dutchman[19] (the Obie winner
for 1963-64), far from deploring violence, believes it has a
positive function. An angry black separatist, Jones does not

look forward to the eventual end of racial strife and the assimilation of blacks into the white world, a world he considers sterile and moribund.   He works instead, according
to C. W. E. Bigsby, for "a world in which the present order is inverted. "[20]   He preaches, in his own words, the
necessity of "cutting throats. "[21]

   In Dutchman, a white woman, Lula, enters a subway
train and sits down by Clay, a well-dressed, seemingly ami-
able young Negro.   Through a series of provocative remarks and then hysterical insults, she provokes him to strike
her and then to express, in a blistering speech, his hatred
and contempt for whites.   She then calmly stabs him, has
the other passengers throw his body off the train, and finally,
from a new group of riders entering the car, selects her
next victim, an action similar to that of Nolan's play, which
was produced the same year.

   The play stresses the black man's traditional role as
victim and repeats, in fact, a pattern seen in Green's play:
a white person torments a black until the black responds,
either by talking back or hitting back, whereupon the white
takes his revenge, an act usually sanctioned by the traditionally oppressive system.   The Colonel who beats Abe, for
example, explains that "he had to do it" and implies that
Abe should be grateful he does not call the law.   The fact
that Abe was provoked is never considered (392-393).   In
Dutchman, the other passengers in the coach sit impassively
while Lula taunts and finally kills Clay, then they help her
dispose of the body.

   Despite Jones' insistence on the victimization of the
Negro by whites, and despite his rhetoric elsewhere about
the need to "cut throats, " the play is, it seems to me, am-
biguous about the efficacy of retaliation by blacks.   The play

assumes the superiority of black culture over white, a view
occasionally advanced by white writers as well as black ones.
According to this assumption, the Negro has more vitality,
more awareness, more understanding of the essentials of
life--all symbolized by his vigorous sexuality--than the white
man. The white man, drained of all joy and immediacy by
participation in a system that stresses getting and spending
to the exclusion of other values, "doesn't understand anything
but luxury, " as Clay puts it (33). According to Clay, money,
power, and luxury keep the black man from entering the
white man's world. Ironically, however, these are the same
factors which have made the white man's civilization effete.

Furthermore, because the black man has traditionally
been forbidden to express his hostility to the group which
excludes him, he has, according to Clay's big speech, turned
his rage into art. Vigorous self-assertion and thinly veiled
contempt for "the Man" are the wellsprings of black music
and poetry. Clay asserts that Charlie Parker would never
have written a note if he had "just walked up to East Sixty-
Seventh and killed the first ten white people he saw. " Similarly, Bessie Smith "wouldn't have needed that music" if she
had "killed some white people. " Clay, himself a poet, declares that if he could "bleed" Lula, one poem would vanish
(35).

The problem the play presents is this: if the black
man cuts enough throats, inverts the social order, and gets
a "piece of the action"--money, power, luxury--will he not
then become as enervated and eviscerated as he claims the
white man is? If he is no longer the victim of the white
man's violence, what of the music, poetry, and heightened
sexuality which supposedly flow from his sublimated fury?
Obviously, the answer in <u>Dutchman</u> is not assimilation into

a vacuous white society. But neither is it murdering the op-
pressor and losing the "neurosis" which insures his creativi-
ty, vitality, and humanity. Clearly, however, the play makes
the point that the price blacks pay for their escape from
"sanity" is their continued victimization by violent whites.

Like Dutchman, Charles Gordone's No Place to Be
Somebody, 22 the Pulitzer Prize winner of 1969-70, also suggests that being black, in spite of the many and obvious dis-
advantages, is worth it. The play gathers a group of characters in a saloon--some black, some white, and some of
mixed blood. It assiduously avoids stock black-white relations in its presentation of violence. Most of the characters
are abusive, for violence in this play goes beyond the problem of color. Johnny, the black saloon owner, for example,
abuses his white mistress Dee, finally driving her to suicide;
and Shanty Mulligan, a white man, mistreats Cora, a black
woman, in much the same way.

The play, like Dutchman, accepts the notion of blacks
as superior artists and lovers. Johnny, for example, has
two white mistresses--Dee, a prostitute, and Mary Lou, a
college girl. Both are drawn to him by his vigorous masculinity. Shanty Mulligan, who wants to be a drummer, considers being white a disadvantage and prides himself on his
black soul. He fears, in fact, that Cora, although black,
will sap his talent by reinforcing his whiteness. Another
character, Gabe Gabriel, is light enough to "pass for white, "
but he thinks of himself as black and identifies with his black
heritage. Unfortunately, his sense of black identity is a
professional handicap, and he can hardly earn a living as a
black actor because he does not look Negroid enough.

According to Gabe, blacks are a people whose identity can "only be measured by the struggle, the dehumaniza-

tion, the degradation they suffered" (115). Significantly,
though, no black person in the play wants to be white; but
the whites either want to be black--Shanty and Gabe, for
example--or they strongly gravitate to blacks--like Mary Lou
and Dee. The play suggests, like Dutchman, that being a
member of a persecuted minority results in superior vitality
and sense of self.

Probably better than race relations as an index to a
people's attitude toward violence is their attitude toward war.
Racial violence is usually random and sporadic; but war, because it is organized, can never be spontaneous. It requires
massive public approval and cooperation. All the wars
which have punctuated U.S. history have, of course, been resisted in some quarters, [23] but pacificism, in the period under discussion at any rate, is a relatively minor strain in
American life and a minor strain in prize-winning plays as
well. Most popular plays about war tend to reflect the prevailing attitudes in the country at the time, which means that
most tend to accept war and glorify warriors.

The years between World War I and the outbreak of
hostilities in 1941 were, however, years when pacificism
was a popular, even fashionable, attitude. It is not surprising, therefore, that one of the two anti-war plays to win a
major drama award comes from this period. Edmond Gagey,
who chronicled the theatre history during these years, says
that the American theatre of the times was full of anti-war
sentiment; in fact, playgoers witnessed a "concerted attack
on war and patriotism."[24] Idiot's Delight[25] by Robert E.
Sherwood, the only anti-war play of the period to win a
prize (the Pulitzer in 1935-36), takes note of the horrors of
fascism but unequivocally condemns war as obscene and
childish nonsense, a stage that man must pass through in the

evolutionary march toward full humanity. Unlike The Green
Pastures and Winterset, which seem to say that man is basically violent, Idiot's Delight means to assert that man is
basically good. Since pacifism is a difficult position to
maintain if one's view of man includes his inherent bestiality, Sherwood, in a postscript to the play, proclaimed his
belief that the world "is populated largely by decent people"
who do not want war. They fight and die only because they
have been deluded by their exploiters, "members of an indecent minority." According to Sherwood, people who say
"war is inevitable" are false prophets (921).

The play gathers a motley group of travelers in a
third-rate resort hotel near the border--soon to be closed--
of Austria and Switzerland. The time is just before the
outbreak of the war. Sherwood, having diagnosed the violence in mankind as the result of "the synthetic spirit of
patriotism" (921), makes one of the central themes of the
play the relationship of the characters vis-a-vis nationalism.
Many of them are avowed internationalists--a radical French-
man, Quillery, for example, works in the international labor
movement and claims no nationality. He places his hopes
for peace in the "mature intelligence" of the workers of the
world (874-875). Another character, a German scientist
working on a cancer cure, sees himself as a "servant of
the whole damn stupid race" (866). A foil to the doctor is
Achille Weber, a munitions manufacturer, a merchant of
death. He too, according to his disillusioned mistress
Irene, is above petty nationalism: he will sell arms to any
country.

When the war breaks out, all except Weber revert to
the nationalism they had previously scorned. Quillery, in-
furiated when he hears that Paris has been bombed, de-

nounces the fascists and dies before a firing squad shouting
"Vive la France. " The doctor, who had earlier denounced
war as absurd, goes back to Germany to put his services at
the disposal of his country. Thus the "indecent minority"
seduces otherwise well-meaning people and they regress to a
lower level of behavior.

Despite Sherwood's instence that violence is just a
"phase, " like teething or bedwetting, the play contains some
disquieting clues that suggest that the problem runs deeper
than Sherwood's awareness of it. The pessimistic doctor,
for example, believes that mankind is "diseased. " The
Italian captain says experience has taught him that war is a
fact of human life. The Cherrys, a honeymooning English
couple, deplore war as "bestial frenzy, " yet when someone
makes a slurring remark about England, Cherry is ready to
fight like a schoolboy. As the play ends, he goes back to
England to help "save civilization" (909). Even Harry Van,
an indefatiguable American optimist, although he believes
that people have faith in peace on earth, knows from experience that they have only "meager intelligence" (881). The
play wants to say that war is stupid and childish and, like
the violent games of children, can be left behind if only man
would emerge, finally, from the long Stone Age. Unfortunately, given the greed and cunning of people like Weber,
and the general animal stupidity of all the rest, the play
actually holds out little hope for war's eradication.

In the light of subsequent world developments, Sherwood was unable to maintain his pacifist stance. In fact, a
theme which constantly occupied him after Idiot's Delight was
the point at which appeasement and nonviolence become moral indifference or cowardice. He dealt with the problem in
his next play, Abe Lincoln in Illinois, 26 the Pulitzer Prize

winner of 1938-39. The play shows, in Sherwood's words,
"a man of peace who had to face the issue of appeasement
or war." The mood in Abe Lincoln is one of anguished un-
certainty that violence can ever be justified, but Lincoln finally resolves the issue by sending troops into Fort Sumter.
Sherwood concedes that that gesture did mean war, and for
Lincoln "it meant four years of anguish and then violent
death. But," Sherwood adds significantly, "it saved the
union."27

Sherwood's next play, There Shall Be No Night (1941),
earned him another Pulitzer Prize and the title of "War-
monger" from both the communist and the fascist press. 28
The theme of the play is the need for good, peace-loving
people to take up the sword, however reluctantly, when aggression threatens. In the light of Hitler's frightening rise
to power, Sherwood decided that decent people had to fight
some wars. The play shows the progress of Dr. Kaarlo
Valkonen, a Finnish scientist and Nobel laureate, from militant pacifism to the belief that resistance to aggression is a
moral imperative. Dr. Valkonen, like the doctor in Idiot's
Delight, is a citizen of the world and a servant of the whole
race (79). Both the doctor and his American-born wife
Miranda oppose war on both practical and moral grounds.
They get an opportunity to voice these sentiments when their
son Erik, in the face of the Soviet invasion of Finland,
wants to join the ski troops. Miranda tells him that fighting
will not do any good. Kaarlo says that fighting is a substitute for intelligence. Erik responds with one of the main
theses of the play: "When your enemies are relying on
force, you can't meet them with theories. You can't throw
books at them--even good books. What else can anybody do
but fight?" (63).

The doctor eventually enters the war as a noncom-
batant, in his capacity as a physician.   After the death of
Erik, however, and in the face of the massive Soviet invasion, he dramatically rips off his Red Cross armband,
takes up a gun, and heads for the front, where he is subsequently killed.   Meanwhile, Miranda and Kaarlo's brother
Waldemar, in keeping with the Finnish tradition of resistance
to the last man, make plans to burn the house and make a
last stand in the garden.

Kaarlo's progress from pacifism to moral anguish to
complete certainty that war is necessary follows the evolution
of Sherwood's thinking and, according to Casper Nannes'
Politics in the American Drama, represents in microcosm
the road traveled by many liberals in the U.S. during the
pre-war period. [29]

Another play of the pre-war period which posits the
necessity for good people to resist malignant aggression is
Lillian Hellman's Watch on the Rhine, [30] recipient of the
Drama Critics' Circle Award for 1940-1941.   The play, like
There Shall Be No Night, brings a central character to the
conviction that the totalitarian threat must be resisted with
force.   The protagonist in this play is not a philosopher
like Kaarlo Valkonen, but a charming, somewhat frivolous
member of the American upper class, Fanny Farrelly.   Her
awakening comes when her daughter, Sara Muller, whom
she has not seen for many years, comes home with her
German husband and her three children.   Fanny is shocked
to see that they are threadbare and careworn, obviously well
acquainted with need.   Herr Muller, it develops, is a dedicated anti-fascist, a man who bears the marks of captivity
and torture.   During his visit at Fanny's, he learns of the
capture by the Nazis of some of his colleagues.   He intends

to go back to Germany (and almost certain death) in order
to bargain for their release with money he has collected for
the cause.   When an impoverished Roumanian count, also a
houseguest at Fanny's, tries to blackmail him, Kurt calmly
kills him.   Fanny at first is horrified, but finally, once she
realizes that the world has changed, gives him a large sum
of money and helps him escape.

Kurt, like Kaarlo and like Abe Lincoln, detests violence.   He tells Fanny that he is working for "a world in
which all men can die in bed" (325).   That he fights unwill-
ingly makes the conviction that the enemy must be stopped
seem even more urgent.   In cruder forms of pro-war propa-
ganda, the other side is usually depicted as a race of brutes.
One never sees the Nazis in Watch on the Rhine, but the
point of their cruelty and viciousness is made clear by the
almost religious dedication of Kurt to their defeat.   He is
willing to sacrifice his vocation, his family, his health, and
finally even his life to stop them.

Not all pre-war plays which justify the use of force
against aggression deal specifically with international politics.
William Saroyan's The Time of Your Life, [31] which won both
the Pulitzer Prize and the Circle Award for 1939-40, is set
in a bar in San Francisco, and the events in Europe are in
no way central to its action.   The play, both in its Preface
and in its action and characterizations, urges love, generosity, and the rejection of material values.   It also, however,
insists upon the necessity of meeting force with force.   In
the play, the boozy habitués of Nick's Pacific Street Saloon
are confronted by Blick, a brutal cop who invades the place,
threatens to have it closed, and harasses Kitty Duval, a
prostitute.   When Blick is finally shot by Kit Carson, an old
Indian fighter (he says) and teller of tall tales, everyone is

vastly relieved. The play makes the act seem completely
justified, and the episode dramatizes the exhortation made
in the Preface: "Have no shame in being kindly and gentle,
but if the time comes in the time of your life to kill, kill
and have no regret" (385).

Another play of the period which, without reference
to totalitarianism specifically, asserts that evil must be resisted by force is Thornton Wilder's The Skin of Our Teeth
(Pulitzer Prize, 1942-43). [32] Unlike The Time of Your Life,
Wilder's play does treat war, though not any particular one.
The play is a scrambled and farcical history of the human
race. Its theme--that man shall not only endure but prevail--
is developed by showing the Antrobus family--Every family--
surviving not only the hardships of external nature, like gla-
ciers and flood, but also the difficulties caused by man's
own inherent evil. Man in this play suffers not only from
"cold, earthquakes, plagues, " but from "differences of opinion" (55). The play makes clear, like The Green Pastures
and Winterset, that man's "differences of opinion" spring
from his basic tendency toward violence. Cain (here named
Henry) has been a member of the human family almost from
the beginning. In the early stages of the play, both his
father and mother have hopes that Henry can be reformed,
but the final realization that Henry will never be socialized
makes Antrobus, the inventor of practically everything, despair. He "wants to die, " he exclaims whenever he sees the
mark of Cain on his son's forehead. After one of Henry's
constant aggressive acts, Antrobus cries bitterly: "All of
us, we're covered with blood" (47).

By the end of the play, Henry has become a symbol
for all the traits that decent men must resolve to fight--
anarchy, disorder, selfishness, brutality, and destruction.

Antrobus, realizing that his contributions to the race would
be nullified by the forces Henry represents, puts aside
family feeling and vows to fight and destroy him. In his
final speech, Antrobus declares that "every good and excel-
lent thing in the world stands moment by moment on the ra-
zor-edge of danger and must be fought for--whether it's a
field, or a home, or a country" (140). Life, the play suggests, must be a constant struggle in which good people
stand prepared to battle evil and chaos.

Predictably, plays with mass appeal coming out of
the period just before and during the war tend to glorify
America as the savior of mankind, to vilify the enemy, and
to imply that any means useful in insuring their defeat are
morally acceptable. After the war, however, some plays
attempt to reassess the experience. Many continue, of
course, to accept the nobility of the cause. In fact, many
prize-winning American plays contain scenes in which a man
explains apologetically, often to his son, why he was unable
to serve in the war or get into combat. Frank Gilroy's
The Subject Was Roses (1964-65) and David Rabe's Sticks
and Bones (1971-72) are two examples. Often a noncom-
batant's job in the service is denigrated, as in Mister
Roberts (1947-48).

Some plays celebrate and mourn the victims of war,
for example, the Frances Goodrich-Albert Hackett play, The
Diary of Anne Frank (1955-56). Others ask whether the
sacrifices demanded by the war were worth it, as in Arthur
Miller's All My Sons (1946-47) and Frank Gilroy's Who'll
Save the Plowboy? (1961-62). At least one play calls into
question one of the fundamental assumptions behind violence--
the belief that when one's cause is noble, the end justifies
the means. Sidney Kingsley's play Darkness at Noon, [33] the

Circle Award winner for 1950-51, based on Arthur Koestler's novel of the same name, provides a resounding "no" to the question whether violence is justified even in a good cause.

The protagonist of the play is N. S. Rubashov, former Soviet leader, participant in the overthrow of the Czar, and one-time national hero. Rubashov, now in prison as a deviationist, is forced to review his life and his political philosophy and to judge where his beliefs have led him and his country. The old guard revolutionaries are presented as admirable men, willing to rot in every jail in Europe, to die if necessary for their "golden dream," the dream of a better life for the Russian people. Their zeal, however, made them ruthless, and they embraced violence and brutality as the proper means to their end (509). Rubashov, for example, says that a "bloodless revolution is a contradiction in terms. Illegality and violence are like dynamite in the hands of a true revolutionary--weapons in the class struggle" (517).

Later, however, when the revolution is taken over by a repressive leader who turns violence against the people, Rubashov is forced to admit that the ideology and tactics of his group have produced the breed of new Neanderthals now running the country. Thus the play, in direct contradiction to many plays of the World War II period, denies that "the end justifies the means." It raises instead serious doubts about the morality and practicality of using force even in a just cause.

If one looks at the theatre of the sixties for clues about attitudes toward violence, the evidence seems confusing. The violence in many recent plays, especially those of the avant-garde, has prompted Morris Freedman to label the trend "The New Senecanism." According to Freedman,

a number of these plays delight merely in the accumulation
of gratuitous horrors. Others, however, are deliberately
designed to shock in order to pierce the defenses of an audience which many playwrights see as morally indifferent to
cruelty and suffering. [34] The violence onstage becomes a
protest, then, against violence itself. Oddly enough, the
plays of the pre-war and war period that insisted on the
morality of war were usually restrained in their presentation of violence. There Shall Be No Night, for example,
contains no physical violence at all. In Watch on the Rhine,
Kurt knocks Teck unconscious onstage but murders him off.
In the sixties, on the other hand, onstage violence becomes
a commonplace in plays which are often bitter anti-war protests. Such a play is David Rabe's Sticks and Bones, [35] a
play of such ferocity that the Columbia Broadcasting System
withdrew the television version because of protests from local stations.

     The play, which won both the Circle Award and the
Tony Award for 1971-72, concerns the return from Vietnam
of a blind veteran, David Nelson, a young man whose war
experiences lead to his alienation from his family. Violence in America is a central theme of the play. David's
family--Ozzie, Harriet and Ricky Nelson (a burlesque of a
television situation-comedy family)--fear David because of
the terrible experiences he has witnessed and because they
suspect that he, too, has "butchered thousands" (183). Under
the tension surrounding David's return, however, Ozzie, the
innocuous stock "Daddy, " cracks and reveals himself as a
man of deeply violent tendencies, heretofore carefully
masked. Ricky, the bland "Hi Mom, Hi Dad" teenager, interested only if girls, food, and the guitar, reveals himself,
finally, as a cold-blooded killer who would murder for fun.

David, on the other hand, is the only sensitive member of
the family.   When he tries to exorcise his nightmares of
Vietnam by making the others understand what happened
there, they refuse to listen.   Finally, in the most horrifying scene of the play, they assist him in committing suicide.
This violent play, so full of venomous disgust and moral
outrage, was written, in the words of one reviewer, "out of
rage over what Rabe ... considers our widespread compla-
cency about the events in Vietnam."[36] Sticks and Bones
thus provides a striking example of a violent play which protests violence.

While Sticks and Bones is generally considered an
anti-war protest, certainly a protest against insensitivity to
war, the play also suggests that the war experience ennobles.
David's searing experiences have given him a capacity for
outrage totally lacking in his banal "sit-com" family.   One
finds the same suggestion in Arthur Miller's All My Sons[37]
(Circle Award, 1946-47).   In this play, Chris Keller experiences a spiritual awakening, the result of his tour of duty
in World War II, and then, like David, has difficulty adjust-
ing to the lower level of intensity at home.   What Chris dis-
covered during the war was brotherhood, "a kind of responsibility, man for man" (31).   He says that if the members of
his company had been a little more selfish, "they'd've been
here today."   Upon his return to the United States, however,
Chris realizes that the civilian population has little understanding of the sacrifices made.   Like David in Sticks and
Bones, Chris is disillusioned when he finds the people back
home wholly preoccupied with material things.   Their lack
of understanding, Chris says, makes "suckers out of a lot
of guys" (32).

The Skin of Our Teeth also contains a character who

finds war a heightened spiritual experience.   Mr. Antrobus,
like Chris, believes that during wartime, people are more
decent: "When you're at war, " he says, "you think about a
better life; when you're at peace you think about a more comfortable one" (135).   The suggestion in these plays is that
on the anvil of war, a finer self is forged.   The obsessions
of bourgeois life are stipped away; the essentials--love and
brotherhood--become central.

Another play which shows violence as a positive value
is John Van Druten's I Am A Camera, which won the Circle
Award in 1951-52.   The protagonist, young Christopher Isherwood, a writer, goes to Berlin in the days preceding the
outbreak of World War II.   In a period of creative paralysis,
Isherwood, in lieu of writing, spends his time merely observing in a detached way everything around him, including the
rise of the Nazis to power.   The end of his period of drought
is signaled when he gets into a street fight with a gang of
Nazis who were harassing one of his Jewish students.   Violence in this play is a symbol of moral regeneration, an indication that one is a fully human participant in life.   Nonviolence, on the other hand, is moral passiveness.

Several plays show violence as an act of kindness or
mercy.   In William Gibson's The Miracle Worker (Tony
Award, 1959-60), Annie Sullivan, the teacher of Helen Keller,
realizing that the child is little more than an undisciplined
animal, begins her seemingly impossible task by trying to
teach her some table manners.   When Helen throws a temper
tantrum, Annie locks the indulgent family out of the dining
room, and in a pitched battle, in which she repeatedly slaps
the girl and knocks her to the floor, subdues her.   The impression the play gives is that such treatment was long over-
due and that only through violence lies hope for salvation.

Even killing is condoned in Steinbeck's play <u>Of Mice and Men</u>, the Circle Award winner of 1937-38. Here George shoots his moronic sidekick Lennie, an act of mercy, the play implies, which saves him from an angry lynch mob.

The overall impression left by a reading of this entire body of plays is that violence always has been and always will be a conspicuous feature of the social landscape, a regrettable necessity, to be sure, but yet not without opportunities for virtue. Given the inclination to ruthless aggression with which man was probably endowed by his Creator, several plays suggest, any pacifist stance is unrealistic. In fact, the plays in this group which cry out against violence are merely a punctuation in a long series of others which assert or imply that violence, like the poor, will be with us always. Few explore the idea that war is a cultural and social condition which can or ought to be controlled. Few indicate constructive channels for aggression or even suggest alternatives to violent behavior. Thus, while one play glorifies the armed resistance of the Finns against the Soviets, none dramatizes the successful nonviolent resistance of the Norwegians against the Nazis, or the Indians against the British, or the Birmingham Blacks against the white establishment.

Even plays which protest violent solutions to problems tend to show people as always perilously close to employing them. The instant regression of otherwise good people into rabid chauvinistic nationalism in <u>Idiot's Delight</u> is a good example; so is Hatcher Hughes' <u>Hell-Bent fer Heaven</u> (Pulitzer Prize, 1923-24), which shows the reactivation of an ancient feud among mountain folk after only the flimsiest provocation. Men are, many plays suggest, always simmering, simmering. Almost anything can bring them to the boil.

The underlying assumption of many plays, moreover, is that violence is a good and useful way of coping, of clearing the air, of establishing one's identity, one's manhood, one's loyalty to one's country, even of regenerating oneself morally.[38] One psychiatrist has recently said that the "ability to justify any form of violence is part of man's extraordinary cerebral endowment."[39] If this is so, then the typical prize-winning American play amply illustrates that capacity.

NOTES

1. For stunning documentation of the savagery and despair of village life in America, see Wisconsin Death Trip by Michael Lesy (New York: Pantheon, 1973).

2. John Herbers, Introduction to The History of Violence in America: A Report to the National Commission on the Causes and Prevention of Violence (New York: Bantam Books, Inc., 1969), p. xiii.

3. Brown, the young black militant, made this statement in Detroit in 1967. The statement is central to his thought and is reproduced on the dust cover of his autobiography Die Nigger Die! (New York: The Dial Press, 1969).

4. Frederic Wertham, M.D., A Sign for Cain: An Exploration of Human Violence (New York: Warner Books, Inc., 1969), p. 313.

5. A New Edition of the Pulitzer Prize Plays, ed. Kathryn Coe and William Cordell (New York: Random House, 1940), pp. 599-648.

6. Brooks Atkinson, cited in John Mason Brown's Dramatis Personae (New York: Viking Press, 1963), p. 15.

7. For a provocative discussion of Connelly's characterization of God and its social and moral implications, see Paul T. Nolan's "God on Stage: A Problem in Characterization," Xavier University Studies, IV (May,

1965), 75-84; and his "Marc Connelly's 'Divine Comedy': Green Pastures Revisited, " Western Speech, XXX (Fall, 1966), 216-224.

8. (Washington: Anderson House, 1935).

9. "Shakespeare in Winterset, " Educational Theatre Journal, VI (1954), 246-247.

10. Ibid., 247.

11. This play, winner of the Players' Workshop Award in 1963-64, was subsequently published in an actor's edition in 1971 and in a reader's edition with an introduction in 1973 by The Edgemoor Press of Houston, Texas, under the title The Loneliest Game.

12. (New York: Farrar, Straus, and Giroux, 1964).

13. Ibid., p. xii.

14. The Naked Image (New York: The Macmillan Co., 1966), p. 96.

15. History of Violence in America, p. 63.

16. The third of the one-act plays, "Endecott and the Red Cross, " was dropped before opening night.

17. Valerie B. Levy, Unpublished dissertation entitled Violence as Drama: A Study of the Development of the Use of Violence on the American Stage (Claremont, 1970), p. 154.

18. A New Edition of the Pulitzer Prize Plays, pp. 381-426.

19. Dutchman and The Slave (New York: William Morrow & Co., 1964).

20. Confrontation and Commitment: A Study of Contemporary American Drama, 1959-1966 (Univ. of Missouri Press, 1967), p. 142.

21. "Brief Reflections on Two Hot Shots, " Kulture, III (Winter, 1963), 3-5.

22. (New York: Bobbs-Merrill Co., 1969).

23. The History of Violence in America, pp. 529-550, contains a discussion of the history of anti-war sentiment in America.

24. Revolution in American Drama (New York: Columbia Univ. Press, 1947), p. 128.

25. A New Edition of the Pulitzer Prize Plays, pp. 859-921.

26. Ibid., pp. 1029-1091.

27. Introduction, There Shall Be No Night (New York: Charles Scribner's Sons, 1940), p. xxiii.

28. Caspar Nannes, Politics in the American Drama (Washington, D.C.: The Catholic University Press, 1960), p. 156.

29. Ibid., p. 159.

30. Four Plays by Lillian Hellman (New York: Random House, 1942).

31. Famous American Plays of the 1930's (New York: Dell Publishing Co., 1959), pp. 385-480.

32. (New York: Harper and Bros., 1942).

33. Best American Plays, 1945-1951, ed. John Gassner (New York: Crown Publishers, Inc., 1952), pp. 505-545.

34. American Drama in Social Context (Carbondale: So. Illinois Press, 1971), pp. 99-110.

35. The Basic Training of Pavlo Hummel and Sticks and Bones: Two Plays by David Rabe (New York: Viking Press, 1973), pp. 113-214.

36. David Watt, The New York Daily News, Nov. 8, 1971.

37. (New York: Reynal and Hitchcock, 1947).

38. A recent study of violence in America suggests that be-

cause the colonists had to tear a country out of the
wilderness in order to regenerate their fortunes and
the power of their church and country, the "myth of
regeneration through violence became the structuring
metaphor of the American experience." See Richard
Slotkin, Regeneration Through Violence: The Mythology of the American Frontier, 1600-1860 (Middleton,
Conn.: The Wesleyan Univ. Press, 1973), p. 5.

39. Violence and the Struggle for Existence, ed. David N.
Daniels, Marshall F. Gilula, and Frank M. Ochberg
(Boston: Little, Brown and Co., 1970), p. 428.

Chapter 4

POLITICS

Because men are generally political animals, the
drama they created became early a vehicle for comment
upon governments, those who make them, those who support
them, and those who merely endure them. Indeed, it is difficult to think of many periods in which the theatre does not
reflect this enduring concern. According to Arthur Hobson
Quinn, the plays of nineteenth century America did not, [1] but
modern America has amply corrected the deficiency. Lit-
erally hundreds of twentieth-century plays have a specifically
political theme; feature real or imagined political characters;
revolve around some contemporary political event; explore
political philosophies; point out abuses of power; or denounce
--overtly or by implication--weaknesses in the political system. Many other plays which do not deal directly with political characters or situations, do reveal attitudes about the
American political system.

That many, indeed most, of the plays which treat
politics are ephemeral, written out of the heat of the moment, designed to capitalize upon public interest in a topi-
cal event, is obvious to anyone concerned with drama. Perhaps no American play will endure with Aristophanes' satires
or Shakespeare's chronicles as timeless examples of political drama. Artistic merit, however, is of less concern

here than is the reflection of popular ideas about or popular interest in American politics.

The prize-winning plays--recipients of major drama awards between 1917 and the present--which deal specifically with politics all reveal attitudes about: 1) individual politicians, 2) the political process, and 3) the electorate. Although the view of the individual politician and of the electorate may vary from one play to another, all of the prize-winning American plays insist upon the corrupt and corruptive nature of politics itself. No play in this group refutes the commonplace American attitude that politics is dirty business.

In the four plays which are about actual politicians-- Thomas Jefferson, Abraham Lincoln, Franklin Roosevelt, and Fiorello La Guardia--the touchstone for the ideal politician is established. Each of these plays presents the politician as hero, as secular saint, tempted but undefiled by a system which, on the one hand, requires enormous amounts of energy, self-sacrifice and commitment; but which on the other, is fraught with situations which require compromise of principle.

One can discern from the characterizations in these four plays the fundamental attributes of the good political hero, as opposed to the merely good politician. Generally, he must be modest and display some reluctance in seeking office; he must have a vision of what he wants the country to be; he must have faith in the people he seeks to govern; and he must be a devoted family man. The protagonists of these four plays are all consistently, monotonously, predictably noble. In fact, no prize-winning play to date depicts a politician with any complexity, as Robert Penn Warren, for example, portrays Huey P. Long in All the King's Men.

A view of the earliest workings of government in
America is presented in Sidney Kingsley's Circle Award play
of 1942-43, The Patriots. [2] Its protagonist, Thomas Jefferson, is the prototypical political hero.   Something of a
Christ-figure, in fact, he has a compelling sense of mission
and suffers agonizes for the people he serves.   Indeed, his
face, according to the stage directions, is at one point trans-
figured by an almost "sacred" light (331).   Although his
talents are considerable, so is his modesty.   He is at first
reluctant to take the job as Secretary of State which Washington urges upon him.   He fears, he confides to his daughter,
that Nature did not make him for office (338).   His sense of
public service is acute, however, and although he longs to
return to Monticello as a gentleman farmer (much as Washington is said to long for his life at Mount Vernon), his intense desire to see the success of the American experiment
--"the last, best hope of the world"--keeps him at his post.
When in the closing moments of the play, he is elected
President, he accepts the office with misgivings, calling it
"a glorious misery" (376).   Over and over, the play stresses
the enormity of his personal sacrifice.

Jefferson's qualities are emphasized by the presence
in the play of his foil, Alexander Hamilton.   While Jefferson's concept of public service drives him to accept office
at great cost to himself, Hamilton, the play suggests, used
politics to further himself socially and financially.   While
Jefferson was unshakably honest, Hamilton did not shrink
from machinations of dubious morality to achieve his ends.
For example, he offers to deliver the presidency into Jefferson's hands in return for concessions later, but Jefferson
refuses without hesitation.   The play also presents Jefferson as a family man, devoted to his daughters and to the

memory of his dead wife.   Hamilton, on the other hand, is
exposed as a philanderer.

Perhaps the most compelling difference between the
characters of Jefferson and Hamilton is the way each views
the common man.   Emphatically Jefferson, the great demo-
crat, voices his faith in the people.   In fact, the climax of
the play consists of his ringing tribute to the American
people who, he says, will never submit to tyranny (359).
Only once does he falter in his belief that the people are
capable of governing themselves.   Later, he declares that
the leaders failed the people and not the other way around.
Hamilton, by way of contrast, states that democracy is a
"philosophic experiment" that failed (361).   His insistance
that a moneyed aristocracy should run the country makes
him indifferent to the plight of the common man, of whom
he holds a low opinion.

Kingsley takes pains to show that Hamilton's estima-
tion is wrong.   In its relentless glorification of the common
man, the play brings forward from time to time servants,
stable boys, blacksmiths, soldiers, and frontiersmen in order to demonstrate that they are not rabble but are reasonable, well-informed and above all, passionately committed
to protecting their new-found liberty.   Thus, The Patriots
insists that the public is not at all the "great beast" that
Hamilton proclaimed it to be (365).

According to Allan Lewis, this play, produced during
World War II, was intended to "encourage renewed faith in
the American destiny, "[3] a fact which may explain the heavily
romanticized view of both the democratic system, the politician, and the electorate.   Significantly, however, the play
still presents politics itself as unsavory.   Unimpeachably
honest himself, even Jefferson is a constant target for abu-

sive attacks, scurrilous satires, and whispered lies. "Politics," he cries at one point, "destroys the happiness of
everyone in this city." He feels himself surrounded by
"rank and malignant hatreds." Referring to political life,
he exclaims in a moment of disgust, "This isn't spending
one's life, it's getting rid of it" (358). The Patriots is,
moreover, only one of many American plays which shows a
decent man trying to survive in a system in which decency
is not a requirement but a handicap.

An earlier play which treats a later political hero is
Robert E. Sherwood's Abe Lincoln in Illinois, [4] the Pulitzer
Prize play of 1938-39. This play resembles The Patriots
in its treatment of a national hero. Like Jefferson, Lincoln
is a reluctant public servant, modest in his assessment of
his qualifications but energized by his vision of a free and
enlightened society. Like Jefferson, he must be urged to
accept the burden of office. Also like Jefferson, he is a
devoted husband (a more impressive achievement than Jefferson's, for Mrs. Jefferson dies young, while Mary Todd Lincoln is very much alive). Lincoln also shares Jefferson's
faith in the common man and sees America as the last hope
of freedom in the world. On the eve of his departure for
Washington to assume the office of President, he tells the
crowd assembled at Springfield that the Union must be saved,
for if it perishes, man's ancient dream of liberty will per-
ish with it.

Abe Lincoln in Illinois, also like The Patriots, shows
an individual politician who is upright and idealistic trying
to work within a political process which is rife with cynicism, opportunism, and greed. The seamy side of party
politics is exposed in the scene in which the party leaders
come to discuss with Lincoln, who has recently distinguished

himself in the debates with Douglas, the possibility of his
nomination for President.   While Lincoln is out of the room,
the men reveal that they consider him an infidel, a radical,
"as unscrupulous a demagogue as Douglas, " and "a dealer
in humbug" (1081-82).   Nevertheless, he has what they consider the one essential qualification for a potential candidate:
he can win.   "The eternal stupidity of the voters" will, they
believe, insure Abe's victory.   Once he is in the White
House, the politicians assume, they can manipulate him as
they like.

Lincoln, of course, wins the election but emerges
from the campaign completely disillusioned with the party
that elected him.   After his victory, one of the party leaders triumphantly declares, "We've fought the good fight and
we've won. "   Abe contemptuously replies that it was, in his
opinion, "the dirtiest campaign in the history of corrupt
politics. "   Gloomily, he considers all the promises and pay-
offs made in his name.   "I have been gambled all around,
bought and sold a hundred times. "   His supporters concede
that such is the case, but one says blandly, "the fact remains that you're winning" (1806).   Lincoln, however, like
Jefferson, has the Presidency thrust upon him.   Winning is
the last thing he wants.

While the view of the hero and of the political process is much the same in the two plays, the attitude toward
the people is not so uniformly idealistic.   In fact, the common man here is a good deal less decent than he is shown
to be in The Patriots.   At one point, for example, a great
shouting crowd gathers outside Lincoln's headquarters to
await the returns.   They cheer every bulletin, whether the
news is good or bad, with what one character describes as
"a fine, ignorant enthusiasm" (1084).   In a similar scene

in The Patriots, the crowd waiting to hear the outcome of Jefferson's election is sober, respectful, and intensely concerned with the future of the country.

Another play which features a noted politician is the Circle Award play for 1957-58, Dore Schary's Sunrise at Campobello. [5] Here again the protagonist is presented as a hero in unqualified terms, for Franklin Roosevelt, like Jefferson and Lincoln, is portrayed as a man willing to make tremendous sacrifices for his country. In this play, government is corrupt, party politics of questionable integrity, and the voters stupid and selfish; yet Roosevelt fights his way back from a crippling disease and gives up the life of a comfortable country squire to provide the nation an alternative to Teapot Dome and the Depression. A "dedicated progressive, " Roosevelt, like Jefferson, is a man of the privileged class who dreams of a better life for all men. The play, moreover, presents the hero-politician as a devoted father and faithful husband. His now well-publicized adulteries are never even suggested.

While the playwright depicts the politician as a man of principle, politics itself, as is usual in these plays, is shown as somewhat less than ideal. Roosevelt's mother rates politics "one step above garbage collecting" (11-12), and references in the play to Harding, the Teapot Dome Scandal, and Tammany Hall all serve to reinforce the suggestion that politics can be just as malodorous. The play does not suggest that Roosevelt is in any way dishonest himself, but it does imply that compromise and calculation are virtually indispensable tools of the trade. At one point, for example, Eleanor, who takes her husband's place at party functions while he is ill, remarks: "I'm no politician. I have the naive point of view that in public service, one

should pursue principles without calculating the cost." Louis
Howe, Roosevelt's political advisor, says to Roosevelt:
"She's right. She's no politician" (92). This exchange is
meant as a little joke, of course, but it expresses what is
clearly assumed in most plays about politics--that operating
from principle alone is naive.

The public, for which Roosevelt's enormous sacrifice
is presumably being made, is presented in this play as
rather less than deserving. Roosevelt appears to believe
that voters are generally preoccupied with their selfish concerns; yet he does not see them as incorrigible. He believes
that given the proper moral leadership, the public can act in
an enlightened manner. He quotes Woodrow Wilson as saying that the people can be lifted above material things only
once in a generation. For this reason, conservative government is "in the saddle" two-thirds of the time (11). Roosevelt's mission is to provide the moral climate which will
bring out the best in the electorate, however latent it may
be.

The most recent of the four plays dealing with actual
public figures is the George Abbot-Jerome Weidman musical,
Fiorello!6 The play, winner of the Pulitzer Prize for 1959-
60, follows the career of Fiorello LaGuardia from the time
of his entrance into politics until his decision to run a
second time for mayor of New York. His characterization
follows the familiar pattern: he is portrayed as an incor-
ruptably honest and dedicated public servant as well as a
devoted husband. Although he is brasher than Jefferson,
Lincoln, or Roosevelt and has a positive thirst to win, his
ambition springs not from a desire for personal aggrandizement or power, but from his acute social conscience and
his revulsion against the flagrant corruption he sees around him.

Fiorello! focuses attention upon party machinery and is "a sharp attack," according to Caspar Nannes, on the "political shenanigans" of the period. [7] Like Abe Lincoln in Illinois, the play exposes the cynical way in which nominees are chosen, but while Lincoln was selected because his party thought he could win, LaGuardia was permitted to run simply because (the party hacks assumed) any candidate they supported would lose anyway. Incredibly, however, Fiorello wins. At this point, the politicians express dismay, for having given him so little support, they can now expect little in the way of patronage. Their worst fears are confirmed, in fact, for LaGuardia operates almost completely independently and displays a fine contempt for "nickel-and-dime ward heelers." The considerable discomfort he causes his party is summed up in the observation of one: Fiorello, he complains, "won't play ball--not for one minute" (109).

Indeed, the most refreshing aspect of Fiorello's character is his refusal to "play ball," to cut corners, to speak hypocritically. He has, like Eleanor Roosevelt in Sunrise at Campobello, a complete disregard for consequences when principle is involved. That he can get elected and serve effectively in spite of his idealism and moral absolutism makes Fiorello! the most affirmative of the political plays. As Nannes puts it, the play is "an encouraging tribute to our democratic way of life ... proof that integrity and honesty will eventually win if they are combined with tenacity and courage." [8]

The political plays which feature fictitious characters rather than actual public figures are nowhere as optimistic. While a play like Sunrise at Campobello suggests that a man of vision can lead the public forth from its habitual slough of materialism; and one like Fiorello! indicates that an up-

right man can make his way in politics uninfected by its
traditionally acknowledged moral laxness, Maxwell Anderson's
Both Your Houses, [9] for example, asserts that politics is so
corrupt that no honest man can hope to serve effectively.
Both Your Houses, the Pulitzer Prize play for 1932-33, concerns the initiation at the hands of professional politicians
of an idealistic young schoolteacher, symbolically named
Alan McClean, who comes up to Congress from Nevada.

As a member of the Appropriations Committee,
McClean learns that his colleagues have tacked on various
"pork barrel" projects to a bill which would insure his home
state a much needed irrigation project. When the committee,
fearing a Presidential veto of so large a sum, decides to
trim the figure, McClean is torn between one campaign
promise to secure the dam and another to help cut government spending. When he offers to give up the dam in the
interest of economy, several members of the committee,
amused at his naivete, tell him that in Washington, bribery
is the modus operandi. Patronage, not good causes, is what
counts; and Congressmen only vote for appropriations if they
themselves have something to gain. The outraged McClean
vows to defeat the bill. His strategy is to overload it, to
swell it to such proportions that no one would dare sponsor
or vote for so high a figure. His final disillusionment
comes, however, when the monstrous bill passes the House
by more than the two-thirds majority needed to override the
President's veto.

John Mason Brown once observed that this play contains no villains, only victims of a corruptive system. [10]
The victims have, however, been corrupted absolutely. Although most of the politicians Alan meets are adept at mask-
ing their immoral, even criminal practices, one of them,

old Solomon Fitzmaurice, is wonderfully cynical and frank
about the way government functions and does much to further
Alan's political education.

Sol frankly admits that the elected officials are a
"gang of liver flukes, sucking the blood out of the body poli-
tic..." (43). He is himself, in fact, always engaged in trying to turn politics to personal advantage, to use privilege
to help line his pockets. As for political morality, he tells
Alan that there is a simple formula for deciding what is
right or wrong: God, he says, is "always in the money"
(100). Graft, he further explains, is the one great constant
in government. Parties and administrations come and go,
but "graft varies only in amount, not in kind" (161). In
fact, according to Sol, "graft, special privilege, and corruption" are the "sole business of the government" (163).

If one wonders why the government has sunk to such
an abysmal state, the reason is not far to seek. Anderson's play makes clear the link between corruption in government and a selfish public. Some political plays indicate
that the public is too stupid or too apathetic to know or care
what goes on in Washington; this one, however, says that
the voters are just as greedy and immoral as the politicians.
Sol, in a big speech, says that every man in Congress came
up to Washington filled with "high purpose," but because the
voters insist on their "share of the plunder," a politician
must "play ball"; otherwise, he will not stand a chance of
reelection (54-55).

Finally, Alan--Mr. Clean, the idealistic politician--
learns that no one can remain untainted in such a system.
First, he discovers that his own campaign was not managed
honestly. Later, in fighting the appropriations bill, he realizes that in order to beat his colleagues at their own game,

he must employ their tactics.   His secretary, who knows
the ropes, assures him there is no other way to do business.
Completely discouraged, Alan asks if honesty in politics is
possible.   In answer to his question, Simeon Gray, chair-
man of the committee and himself guilty of corrupt practices,
intones the theme of the play: honesty, he says, is "almost
unknown in any government and impossible under our system" (175-176).

Alan's last hope is that the people will finally wake
up and demand better government.   Given the view of the
voting public by such seasoned politicians as Solomon Fitzmaurice, however, Both Your Houses implies that that day
is not yet at hand.   In fact, as Eleanor Flexner observed,
the play treats corruption as "an inevitable appendage of
democracy, "[11] and according to John Mason Brown, Both
Your Houses is "calculated to raise doubts in the hearts of
even the staunchest supporters of the democratic ideal. "[12]

The impact of Both Your Houses was blunted because
it was produced on Broadway only three days after the in-
auguration of Franklin D. Roosevelt.   The country was
clearly expecting better things from Washington; so Anderson was, according to one scholarly observer, "inadvertantly
placed in the position of flogging a horse that had just died
quite publicly. "[13]

That wave of optimism must have spent itself by the
middle forties, for the season of 1945-46 saw the opening of
a play which contained the same theme as Both Your Houses
and proposed the same anemic conclusion.   The play, the
Pulitzer Prize-winner of the season, was State of the Union,
by Howard Lindsay and Russel Crouse. [14]   The protagonist,
Grant Matthews (a thinly disguised Wendell Wilkie, according to Caspar Nannes), [15] is a political babe-in-the-wood,

like Alan McClean of <u>Both Your Houses</u>. Like McClean's,
too, Grant's introduction to practical politics is a shattering
revelation.

The contrast between Grant, a wealthy industrialist,
and the politicians who want him to run for President is il-
luminating. He has a vision of what he wants the country
and the world to be; they are simply looking for a viable
and attractive candidate. He wants to go out and sell himself to the voters by stating his beliefs frankly; they urge
him to speak in generalities, avoiding controversy. He
wants to appeal to the best in people, provide moral leadership, tell them hard truths; they want him to make vague
promises to various pressure groups. He thinks there is
not enough difference between the two parties; they say cynically that the party that gets in is vastly different from the
one that is out. He has Jefferson's faith in the public's intelligence and fundamental good will; they see the voters as
"just people," too ignorant and lethargic to know or care
what goes on.

As in the old moralities, Grant has his good and bad
angel. Mary, his wife, who is even more idealistic than
he, encourages him to act independently and makes him un-
comfortable when he equivocates. His mistress, a rather
brittle and aggressive woman (significantly named Kay
Thorndyke), is a newspaper publisher and a part of the
world of professional politics. In league with party hacks,
her function is to make Grant amenable to compromise and
finally deliver him into the hands of the party leaders, a
suitably malleable candidate at last.

Like most other political heroes in these plays, Grant,
afraid he does not have the qualifications to lead the country,
is at first reluctant to consider running. Once he gets the

bit between his teeth, however, his enthusiasm begins to
build.   At this point, he begins to compromise his principles
in the name of expediency.   Like so many of these plays,
State of the Union implies that the only decent politician is
a man who does not really want the job.   Being "on the
make" politically, having a thirst for power, leads inevitably to moral ambivalence if not outright dishonesty.

This play also spells out what many others have suggested: the good politician must be a good family man.
The electorate expects one to be a faithful husband.   Because Grant and Mary have been estranged (since his affair
with Mrs. Thorndyke), party leaders fear that the public
will reject him.   Consequently, Mary is encouraged to accompany Grant on a speaking tour designed to dispel any
rumors.   According to Jim Conover, the leader of the fac-
tion pushing Grant's nomination, the public expects to see a
candidate's wife by his side.   The cross-country tour designed to present Grant and Mary as a happily married
couple is one of the play's many examples of party manipu-
lation of public opinion.   Appearance, not reality, image,
not substance, the play suggests, is what matters to the
kingmakers.

The play ends when Matthews rebels against Conover
and abandons his chance for the nomination, an act which
suggests that in politics a man must either depart from his
ideals or give up all hope of public service.   Conover sums
it up, using the now familiar metaphor: "to play politics,
you have to play ball" (502).

State of the Union, although exposing the problem of
dishonesty in politics, suggests only the same vague solution as Both Your Houses--a vigilant, informed, honest electorate must rise up and throw the rascals out.   Since most

politicians seem to be incorrigible, the people must take command. "Nobody," Grant tells Mary (to whom he has returned, another sign of his moral regeneration), "can afford to be out of politics" (503). Because he cannot maintain his integrity inside the established framework of party politics, Grant intends to operate independently outside of it. The play vaguely suggests that the party may have to accept Grant Matthews on his own terms, in which case the outcome would be something like the situation in Fiorello! The party would have to bend to the will of the honest candidate. Such a possibility, however, is merely hinted in State of the Union.

An even more cynical view of the American political system is presented in the first musical ever to win a Pulitzer Prize, Of Thee I Sing, the 1931-32 play by George Kaufman and Morrie Ryskind.[16] This play, like the others, hammers out the unfamiliar themes of corruption in government and apathy among the voters; it varies from the pattern, however, by not having a protagonist who struggles valiantly to maintain his integrity in the midst of grasping politicians. John P. Wintergreen, Candidate for President, is no better than his supporters. Like them, he is eager to find a noncontroversial issue on which to base his campaign. Because all the world is popularly supposed to love a lover, Wintergreen and his advisors agree to stage a beauty contest, the winner of which John will marry. Wintergreen, however, almost wrecks the scheme by falling in love with Mary, his secretary. John and Mary salvage the campaign by conducting their courtship publicly; he proposes and she accepts in each of the forty-eight states. Naturally, they win the day.

After being swept into office by a commanding ma-

jority, John's position is threatened when the jilted contest-
winner, Miss Diana Devereaux, makes trouble. Since no one
can ever remember the Vice-President, John's impeachment
would be a double disaster for the party. In a desperate attempt to distract the public, Mary announces her impending
motherhood. With "posterity just around the corner, " John
again becomes the national hero. Miss Devereaux wins as a
consolation prize the forgettable Vice-President, Alexander
Throttlebottom.

This play is not only a tart satire on the vacuity and
gullibility of the electorate; it also gibes at politicians--their
shabby deals, their hypocrisy, their refusal to run on
issues, their meaningless slogans, their cynical willingness
to do anything to get elected. Apparently, the play touched
a national nerve. According to Caspar Nannes, it was received with glee by a Depression-weary public because it
"put into concrete terms the critical feelings people had but
could not so well express. "[17]

Critical feelings about the American political system,
judging from the evidence presented in prize-winning drama,
are widespread. Few plays offer anything but heavily qualified acceptance of the political process, while dozens contain passing references to high taxes, the "mess in Washington, " corruption in high places, junketing Congressmen,
ponderous Southern senators, and stupid voters. A witti-
cism here, a complaint there, but taken altogether they constitute a litany of skepticism and distrust.

Oddly enough, in spite of the deep malaise expressed,
solutions are seldom suggested. Few plays imply that legislation can cure social ills, and in spite of the fact that many
of these playwrights have been considered left of center, no
prize-winning play advocates Marxism or even mild forms

of socialism. Street Scene, for example, written by the
deeply committed liberal Elmer Rice, posits situations--pov-
erty and substandard housing, to mention only two--which
could be alleviated by legislation. In this play, however,
Rice does not advance any particular economic or political
philosophy. As one student of his work notes, in Street
Scene Rice is only a "propagandist ... for the human spirit,
the worth of the individual. "[18] As in so many of these
plays, a vague hope of reform emerges but no concrete solutions. Several plays, Both Your Houses and State of the
Union, for example, issue a clarion call for people to wake
up, but wake up and do what, exactly, is never quite clear.

This reluctance to suggest solutions could be written
off as simply a failure of the imagination or a reluctance to
propagandize for specific causes. The plays themselves,
however, suggest several other possibilities. One is utter
despair of any political solution to any problem. What hope,
many playwrights ask, beyond a general reform of human
nature, can politics offer? Such playwrights imply that
given the greed, selfishness, and violence of man, political
solutions are necessary. At the same time, however, those
very traits that necessitate political solutions also nullify the
hope that the political system designed to alleviate social
ills will work. The system is itself so corruptive that any
man who can get elected and stay in office is almost certain
to be corrupted himself. Injustice and dishonesty are the
inevitable results.

One play which gives a particularly clear statement
of this problem is Sidney Kingsley's Men in White, the Pulitzer Prize winner in 1933-34.[19] The theme of this play is
that a doctor's life must be dedicated only to healing. Family considerations, friends, and particularly concern with

money must be ruthlessly subordinated. The play shows
several doctors who succumb to the lure of money, for according to one, worry over money is the one disease a doctor is not trained to fight. One obvious way to free doctors
from money problems--too much as well as too little--is
some form of socialized medicine. Indeed, one doctor says
wistfully that "maybe some day the State will take over
medicine...." Straight the answer comes back from one of
his colleagues: "Before we let the State control medicine,
we'd have to put every politician on the operating table and
cut out his acquisitive instincts." They agree that it would
take "a major operation" (822).

Another possible explanation for the reluctance of
playwrights to advocate specific reforms is that, while the
plays depict social and economic problems that could perhaps be ameliorated through legislation, most of the difficulties shown lie too deep for political solutions. Govern-
ment-run homes for runaway prostitutes are not the answer
in Anna Christie; social security benefits and fair employ-
ment practices are not the answer in Death of a Salesman;
orthopedic care for low-income families is not the answer
in The Glass Menagerie; programs for the mentally retarded
are not the answer in Of Mice and Men. Nearly all plays go
beyond a description of the social and political landscape--
they describe the human condition, for which, all the plays
agree, there is no easy cure.

Although, on the one hand, the general attitude
toward the benefits of political action would suggest despair,
on the other hand, there is also a suggestion that the American system and a meaningful existence can exist and flourish without the hindrance, or aid, of political institutions.
One could argue, of course, that the suspicion of govern-

ment reflected in the prize-winning plays of America is traditionally American, finding its roots in the Declaration of Independence: "... whenever any Form of Government becomes destructive of these ends [securing human rights] it is the Right of the People to alter or to abolish it, and to institute new Government.... Prudence, indeed, will dictate that Governments long established should not be changed for light and transient causes; and accordingly all experience hath shewn, that mankind are more disposed to suffer, while evils are sufferable, than to right themselves by abolishing the forms to which they are accustomed."

The anti-political attitude in these plays, however, is probably less the result of such an American assumption than it is of the form of the American drama itself, a disposition toward a personal realism in which the protagonist is saved, or lost, because of personal virtues or vices, in which matters that are essentially sociological and political are viewed as an individual characterization. In Miller's Death of a Salesman, for example, it is not the "system" that makes Willy a victim and Charlie successful; it is, rather, the individual differences in these two men. As Charlie, himself, comments in the Requiem scene, the things that a decent society can provide ("He only needed a little salary") are not enough.

American drama, at least as it was approved by major prizes, seeks personal achievement and personal fulfillment. It is thus, by its very nature, opposed to political or sociological solutions. The general cynicism toward the political process, it should be noted, is seldom matched by any call for radical change in general assumptions, and the general distrust of the system is seldom made a rejection of the nation that created that system.

NOTES

1. _A History of the American Drama_, I (New York: Harper and Bros., 1927), p. 146.

2. _The Critics' Prize Plays_ (Cleveland: World Publishing Co., 1945), pp. 323-377.

3. _American Plays and Playwrights of the Contemporary Theatre_, rev. ed. (New York: Crown Publishers, 1970), p. 148.

4. _A New Edition of the Pulitzer Prize Plays_, ed. Kathryn Coe and William Cordell (New York: Random House, 1940), pp. 1029-1091.

5. (New York: Random House, 1957).

6. (New York: Random House, 1960).

7. _Politics in the American Drama_ (Washington: The Catholic University of America Press, 1960), p. 223.

8. _Ibid._, p. 218.

9. (New York: Samuel French, 1933).

10. _Two on the Aisle_ (New York: W. W. Norton, 1938), p. 210.

11. _American Playwrights: 1918-1938_ (New York: Simon and Schuster, 1938), p. 126.

12. _Two on the Aisle_, pp. 208-209.

13. John L. Toohey, _A History of the Pulitzer Prize Plays_ (New York: The Citadel Press, 1967), p. 109.

14. _Best American Plays: Third Series 1945-1951_, ed. John Gassner (New York: Crown Publishers, Inc., 1952), pp. 455-503.

15. _Politics in American Drama_, pp. 222-223.

16. _The Pulitzer Prize Plays_, pp. 693-743.

17. _Politics in the American Drama_, p. 105.

18. Frank Durham, Elmer Rice (New York: Twayne Pub-
     lishing Co., 1970), p. 67.

19. The Pulitzer Prize Plays, pp. 795-847.

Chapter 5

RELIGION

Ambivalence about religion has long been a staple ingredient of American culture. Although religion played a fundamental part in shaping the society, and although Americans are quick to invoke religious values into almost any activity (football, for example), American people from their earliest history have also been suspicious of religion. Few politicians dare profess atheism, it is true; yet the Constitution in the strongest terms insures against the religious interpretation of public affairs. Every president must have his Norman Vincent Peale, his Cardinal Cushing, or his Billy Graham in attendance often enough to lend a religious tone to his administration, but Church and State are rigidly separated. Few people in America confess to having no church affiliation, yet nothing can obscure the fact that at bottom, American values are secular, and the characteristic American turn of mind, if not always rational, is seldom spiritual. Max Lerner summed up the religious ambiguity which cuts across the American grain when he wrote that "America is as secular as a culture can be where religion has ... been intertwined with the founding and meaning of the society." At the same time, he continues, the country is "as religious as a culture can be whose life goals are worldly and whose daily strivings revolve not around God but around man."[1]

114

Another characteristic of religion in America is its disunity. While religion in many nations has been a unifying and cohesive force, the religious experience in America is marked by fragmentation and individualism. Perhaps this diffuseness explains why other cultures have produced great religious plays, but the American soil seems incapable of supporting a religious drama. Indeed, among our most respected plays (plays which have won major drama awards since 1917) only one, T. S. Eliot's The Cocktail Party, subordinates drama to religious dogma. Two, The Green Pastures by Marc Connelly and J. B. by Archibald MacLeish, treat conventional religious materials but subordinate religious values to the "humanistic heresy." Indeed, an examination of prize-winning American drama of the twentieth century reveals a consistent tendency on the part of playwrights to urge that conventional concepts of God be discarded in favor of secular humanism.

It is, I think, significant that the one truly religious prize-winning play in American dramatic literature is not solidly in the American mainstream. The Cocktail Party[2] was written long after T. S. Eliot had become more British than the British. The scene is "laid" in London; the characters are mostly fashionable members of that town's upper class; and the dramatic form, the comedy of manners, is an outgrowth of a sophisticated and highly artificial civilization, and not a characteristically American expression. In fact, the only American thing about this play is a reference to California. The assumption then that America has even one orthodox religious play among its most popular drama is open to question.

That the play's intent is religious, even didactic, is not, however, open to question. In The Cocktail Party,

Eliot daringly uses the drawing room comedy, that most
secular of dramatic forms, to explore "the multiple mean-
ings of Christian love and marriage."[3]   The love intrigues
and marital battles so familiar from the high comedy of the
Restoration are provided in this play by Lavinia and Edward
Chamberlayne, the traditionally faithless husband and wife.
Edward is having an affair with Celia Coplestone, Lavinia
with Peter Quilpe.   The situation is further complicated because Peter loves Celia rather than Lavinia, and Edward
loves no one but Edward.   Eliot has these unhappy characters led to a better understanding of themselves and of the
meaning of life by a group of "guardians," Julia Shuttle-
thwaite, Alexander MacColgie Gibbs, and Sir Henry Harcourt-
Reilly.   These characters also function, as Carol Smith observes, as predictable comic stereotypes, "the dowager
eager for gossip, the aging playboy, and the understanding
friend of the family who acts as confidant."[4]

These guardians help the Chamberlaynes to accept
themselves without illusion and then to find happiness in a
more Christian relationship.   Celia, however, is made of
finer spiritual stuff than Edward and Lavinia.   She discovers
her true vocation, renounces the world, joins an austere
nursing order in Africa, and finally dies at the hands of
hostile natives.   Although Edward and Lavinia's successful
reconciliation suggests one way of "working out one's salvation," the play seems quite medieval in its suggestion that
Celia's path, the way of self-immolation and martyrdom, is
the most heroic and the most ecstatic.   Anything less than
sainthood, Reilly says at one point, is simply "making the
best of a bad job" (126).   Several critics have complained
that if Edward and Lavinia are supposed to represent the
human condition, then Eliot has "loaded the dice" against

it. [5] Whatever the play's defects, however, The Cocktail
Party has the distinction of being the only play in this group
which suggests that the summum bonum of life is "transhu-
manization" (147).

While The Cocktail Party uses dramatic form uncon-
ventionally to make an orthodox religious statement, The
Green Pastures and J.B. both rework traditional stories in
an attempt to redefine the concept of God and his relationship to man. Both suggest that the conventional view of God
is limited and needs readjustment.

In The Green Pastures, the Pulitzer Prize winner of
1929-30, Marc Connelly uses a series of Old Testament
stories to portray a fallible God who makes serious blunders
in his dealings with man, and who finally learns from man
how to be better. Connelly's God, while the "hero" of the
play, is consistently drawn on a reduced scale. Comic
touches throughout the play point up his pettiness and vanity,
his frustrations and doubts.

At the end of the play, after God has given up recalcitrant mankind as a bad job, he learns from Hezdrel,
an obscure Hebrew soldier, the nature of the Creature he
has made. According to Paul T. Nolan, "he is a creature
full of weaknesses, but he tries. He has hope in the midst
of catastrophe, courage in the midst of despair, and compassion in the midst of suffering. "[6] Hezdrel, God's moral
superior, Nolan contends, teaches God that He needs more
insight and sympathy. He learns that He can no longer
reign in majestic isolation but must take on human flesh and
suffer as man does.

J.B., [7] Archibald MacLeish's version of the Job story,
a play which won both the Pulitzer Prize and the Tony award
in 1958-59 and which subsequently received a great deal of

critical attention, also diminishes God and exalts man. By
making a modern businessman a parallel for Job, MacLeish
is able to explore ancient and troublesome theological questions in the light of twentieth-century humanistic thought.
While the Biblical Job was a traditional religious figure
whose blind acceptance of whatever God doles out is the
measure of his faith, J. B. comes to grips with irrational
cruelty in a different way. After the incredible sufferings
inflicted upon him, J. B. "simply pushes God to one side, "
according to Allan Lewis, "accepting His existence as a
fact, but placing his faith in love, which permits man to
create, to live, to suffer, to be himself. " Such a conclusion, in Lewis' view, represents the "application of modern
liberalism to theology. "[8]

MacLeish's device of using a circus tent as a microcosm of the universe is as daring as Eliot's use of the
drawing room comedy in The Cocktail Party and Connelly's
portrayal of God as a black man in The Green Pastures.
MacLeish has two circus vendors, Mr. Zuss and Mr.
Nickles, both ham actors, put on masks and play the parts
of God and Satan. This conceit allows the playwright to
supply a running counterpoint criticism of God, for Nickles
keeps calling attention to Zuss' (God's) pomposity, cruelty,
and bungling. For example, in Scene Eight, after a nuclear
holocaust, Nickles observes that Zuss has made another
blunder: "You hit at one man you blast thousands. " He
reminds Zuss of massacres past and says:

> Now you've fumbled again:
> Tumbled a whole city down
> To blister one man's skin with agony. (614)

Like Connelly's God, whose thunderbolts often missed their
mark, Zuss serves as a reminder that the Old Testament
God was not only cruel, but inefficient as well.

Unlike Connelly's God, who learns to be a God of love and mercy, MacLeish's God-figure simply withdraws at the end of the play, leaving the stage to J.B. and his wife, who will "blow on the coal of the heart" and begin again. The play, as Signi Falk observes, suggests that MacLeish finds the idea of a cruel and inscrutable God who demands unthinking submission to His will an outmoded concept. Like Connelly, MacLeish seems to be searching for a new image of God, one that, in Falk's words, "incorporates love with a sense of responsibility, one that can unite a compassion for others with a concern for the individual spirit."[9] The old God of wrath and vengeance, according to both plays, is dead or fled.

Although The Cocktail Party, The Green Pastures, and J.B. are the only prize-winning plays in which the anagogic intent is central, many others have a good deal to say about religion. In some respects the prize-winning plays of the twentieth century resemble the melodramas of the nineteenth, which, according to one scholarly observer, often used religious forms without ever developing a religious theme. Religion, he writes, "was clearly an adjunct to some other topic ... with which the play was centrally concerned."[10] Modern plays, for example, often use religion to promote humanistic social goals, particularly to urge greater tolerance, sympathy, and understanding for ethnic groups. One striking difference between modern plays and those of the past century lies, however, in the efficacy of the God invoked. The God of the melodramas was shown to act directly in the affairs of men, punishing the villainous and rewarding the pure in heart.[11] In most twentieth-century plays, however, the God being petitioned is either deaf or completely disinterested. That a particular group

could believe in such a God and implore his help is one of
the reasons we sympathize with it.

In plays about blacks, for example, sympathy is often
created for Negroes who must, like J.B., try to understand
why the God they love and worship seems to have singled
them out for extraordinary pain. Berenice, the family cook
in Carson McCullers' Circle winner of 1949-50, The Member of the Wedding, [12] is a good example of a person who
believes explicitly in a God who never answers her prayers.
She is the classic mammy, familiar from so much Southern
literature--wise, loving, patient, enduring, and devoutly
Christian. Her life has been one of hardship and great
personal sorrow. Matter of factly and without self-pity she
admits, "All my life I've been wantin' things that I ain't
been gettin' " (179). She describes in one particularly moving speech how she held her husband Ludie in her arms all
night and prayed that he would not die, but he died just the
same. Likewise, she begs God not to take her son, but he,
too, dies. Still, to doubt God is not in her vocabulary of
responses, and her faith is seemingly unshakable.

Such blind faith in an inscrutable God is a characteristic of many older blacks in these plays. Plays which
feature younger blacks struggling to understand their suffering often end, significantly, as J.B. ends: the blacks come
to put their faith not so much in God as in man.

In Abraham's Bosom[13] by Paul Green (Pulitzer Prize
for 1926-27), is the earliest play to show the black man
moving toward humanism. Although the play is centrally
concerned with the unsuccessful struggle of a black man,
Abraham McCranie, to become a leader of his people, it
makes a statement about religion and blacks which was to
be repeated in later plays. It says that blacks of the older

generation accept without question the God who has destined
them for a lowly position in the society. Like the peasant
of the Middle Ages, they believe that to question the justice
of the divine order which ordained their inferior status is to
invite disaster. Younger blacks, however, begin to put their
trust in human betterment.

The views of the more primitive blacks are exemplified in the character of Abraham's old aunt, called Muh
Mack. She tells Abe, for example, that his troubles--crop
failures, the death of his children--are visited upon him because his pride and his grandiose schemes to help blacks
rise are contrary to God's will. She constantly urges him
to humble himself before the Lord and accept his lot without
complaint.

Abe, on the other hand, insists that the notion that
whites were intended by God to be superior to blacks is a
lie. He believes that through education blacks can be led
out of bondage, and to this vision he consecrates his life and
that of his infant son. Clearly, he expects both God and the
white man to help further his cause. He is, of course, dis-
abused of this notion by the end of the play, when his dream
lies shattered and he is about to die at the hands of a lynch mob.

Only once in the play, in a moment of despair, does
he revert to his aunt's position. Here he cries out that the
blacks are down, while the white man is "settin up wid God,
up dere in his favor." He concludes that there is no god
for blacks--"dat's white man's God." When the horrified
women, his aunt and his wife Goldie, tell him that God is
trying to humble him, he points out that many Negroes pray,
pay a preacher, go to church, and are humble. "What do
God do?" he asks. "Starve 'em to deaf. Kill em off lak
flies..." (398).

This bitter speech reflects the nadir of Abe's faith.
Later, after Goldie delivers her first healthy son, Abe re-
pents of his blasphemies, but he does not "humble down" as
the women have urged him to do.   Instead, he prays to the
God of both blacks and whites to sanctify his mission.   He
then offers his son as "a new Moses" to help lead the black
man out of sin, ignorance, and bondage.   Evidently, however, the God he invokes is as indifferent as Connelly's God
before his reconciliation with man, for Abe's inability to
find a place in which to make his contribution to the world,
his abject poverty, his disappointment in his son are all in
spite of his faith.

A repetition of this pattern of blind faith in one generation moderating to the quest for social betterment in the
next can be seen in Lorraine Hansberry's A Raisin in the
Sun,[14] the Circle Award winner in 1958-59.   In this play the
mother, Lena Younger, is staunchly and conventionally
Christian.   She disapproves of liquor, gambling, using the
Lord's name lightly, and reciting Scripture ironically.   While
nowhere so passive as the aunt in In Abraham's Bosom,
Lena seems to accept that the Negro was called to a certain
station in life which he should not try to escape.   She quotes
her husband as having said, "Seem like God didn't see fit to
give the black man nothing but dreams..." (33).

Her money-hungry son, Walter Lee, refers to this
attitude as the "slave mentality."   Although Walter Lee for
most of the play is interested simply in his own advancement
and aggrandizement, his younger sister Beneatha, like Abraham McCranie, wants to make the world better.   Unlike Abe,
however, Beneatha has lost faith in a God she considers ineffectual if not nonexistent.   In an explosive confrontation
with Lena, Beneatha declares that she is tired of hearing

about God--"He doesn't pay tuition." After this outburst
Lena slaps her daughter's face and forces her to say, "In
my mother's house there is still God" (38-40). Beneatha,
undaunted, still believes that curing the sick is "truly being
God" (112). Also a contrast to Lena's conventional religion
is the humanism of Beneatha's sweetheart, an African prince
named Asagi. He says that he "has the religion of doing
what is necessary in the world--and of worshipping man--
because he is so marvelous..." (114).

A recent play in which an emerging black humanism
is presented is Howard Sackler's The Great White Hope.[15]
This play, based on the career of Jack Johnson, the Negro
boxer, swept the field in 1968-69, capturing the Pulitzer
Prize, the Circle Award, and the Tony. More strongly
than any other, The Great White Hope makes the point that
"nigger praying" is not the way for blacks to advance. Jack
(called Jack Jefferson in the play) holds this view, but the
point is nailed down in several scenes by the presence of a
mysterious character named Scipio, identified only as a
street philosopher. His function is to appear at those times
in the play when the more primitive blacks are petitioning
God in their usual way. Invariably, he heaps scorn upon
them for "moaning low" for two hundred years, praying to
the white man's God while the white man oppresses them.
As Scipio puts it, the white man is "pulling de teeth" out of
their heads while the preacher is giving them "de laughing
gas" (144). Whenever disaster strikes, according to him,
the "black flies" just "light down together and hum pretty
please to white man's Jesus" (71). He further jeers at their
misappropriation of the Judeo-Christian tradition, making believe they are "de chillun of Isrel, fiery furnacing and roll-
on Jordanin..." (145). In this play, as in The Member of

the Wedding and In Abraham's Bosom, petitioning the Lord
is completely ineffective.   At one point, for example, Mrs.
Jefferson, her pastor, and a group of friends assemble to
pray that Jack will not get a jail sentence after being con-
victed on a trumped-up charge.   He gets three years.   The
Negro preacher's explanation as to why prayers are not
answered seems weak: "He works in His own way, " he explains, "He ain't juss on tap evvy time we give a holler"
(143).

Criticism of conventional piety is not limited to plays
about blacks by any means; indeed, it is difficult to think of
any prize-winning play that appears to approve of institution-
al religion.   Almost all plays that feature clergymen, for
example, put them in an unflattering light.   This anti-cleri-
cal strain ranges in intensity from mild satire to bitter in-
vective.

Perhaps the gentlest treatment of a cleric occurs in
the first play ever to win the Pulitzer Prize, Jesse Lynch
Williams' Why Marry? (1917-18), a play which satirizes almost every institution in American life.   The play's central
intent is to ask whether marriage is not an outmoded idea.
In the process of giving a rather heavily qualified "yes, "
Williams also manages to suggest that the Church, too, is
in its dotage.   The clergyman in the play, Uncle Theodore,
is a gentle enough man--sentimental, kind, and idealistic--
but completely conventional and unimaginative.   Furthermore,
his need to eke out a living for his large family (clergymen's
salaries being what they are) causes him to vacillate weakly
between his duty as a Christian and his need to stay in the
good graces of the large contributors.   Even though the
picture of Uncle Theodore is not brutal, the church is exposed as a whited sepulchre, "a kept church" one calls it,

actively engaged with the state in propping up rotting social
structures.

Sidney Howard's They Knew What They Wanted, [16] the
Pulitzer winner in 1924-25, is another play that throws an
unflattering light on a cleric. Here, the basic situation is
that Tony Pattuci, a sixty-year old winegrower, a robust
Italian now living in California, wants to marry Amy, a
young girl in her twenties. Tony's priest, described as
"semi-somnolent, " and "the American counterpart of the
French village curé, " disapproves of the marriage, and indeed, of almost everything. In addition to being puritanical
and rather mean-spirited, Father McKee is identified by his
speeches as an ignorant man. No one in the play takes him
seriously; in fact, most of the characters are quite disre-
spectful. Tony, for example, pays absolutely no attention
to his advice. Joe, Tony's foreman, a one-time labor organizer, rudely challenges him on a point of theology by
saying "a helluva lot you ... know about the life of Jesus"
(285). A doctor in the play calls him a "bigoted old soak"
(301).

Tony, although he is constantly being reproached by
the priest, reveals himself as a truly religious man, not
churchy but on intimate terms with the Lord: "God, " he
says knowingly, "is no cheap fella..." (297). He curses
constantly, even when referring to God, and he is, moreover, intensely superstitious. Nevertheless, Tony is a much
more wholesome and attractive man than Father McKee.

Tennessee Williams is another playwright who takes
a consistently dim view of organized religion, and in his
prize-winning plays that touch on religion--The Rose Tattoo
(Tony Award, 1950-51), Cat on a Hot Tin Roof (Pulitzer
Prize and Circle Award, 1954-55), and Night of the Iguana

(Circle Award, 1961-62)--churches and clergymen are generally presented unfavorably. The Catholic priest in The Rose
Tattoo is drawn with more sympathy than the one in They
Knew What They Wanted, but the basic situation is much the
same. In both plays, the vigorous Mediterranean religion
of the protagonist makes that of the priest seem rather
bloodless. Furthermore, like Father McKee, Father DeLeo
is completely ineffectual. In spite of his warnings and
scoldings, the central figure in the play, Serafina delle
Rose, has the body of her adored husband cremated and his
ashes placed in an urn in her house. Father DeLeo can
neither comfort her nor force her to end the destructive
self-indulgence of her extravagant grief. That he means
well is about the most that can be said in his favor.

The minister in Cat on a Hot Tin Roof[17] is utterly
despicable. When Big Daddy Pollitt, owner of a large plantation, is found to have cancer, the Rev. Mr. Tooker,
called "Preach" by Big Daddy, hovers around hinting about
the expensive memorials other families have donated to the
church. To their credit, the entire family is properly contemptuous of the minister. Big Mama involves him in an
undignified bit of horseplay, and Big Daddy is given to such
pungent expressions as "Rut the goddam preacher!" (58).
In spite of his contempt for his minister, Big Daddy has always been a churchgoer and has behaved in accordance with
the social conventions. The church, however, is hardly a
force in his life; in fact, he confesses that church "bores
the bejeasus" out of him. As he approaches the end of
his life, he wishes he had devoted himself less to respectability and religiosity and more to the pleasures of
the flesh.

The attitude toward clergy and church is rather more
complex in Night of the Iguana[18] because in this play the

protagonist is a clergyman.   The Rev. T. Lawrence Shannon, locked out of his church for fornication and heresy, is
now reduced to the position of tour guide for a third-rate
company in Mexico.   Although he still keeps his gold cross
and plans to petition his Bishop to reinstate him into the
ministry, the possibility of his reentering the church is
never seriously presented in the play.

While conducting the members of a female Baptist
academy through rural Mexico, Shannon finds himself dangerously near another emotional collapse and seeks refuge at
the Costa Verde, a hotel run by his old friend, Maxine,
now a lusty widow.   At the hotel, he also meets Hannah
Jelkes, a New England spinster, and her elderly grandfather,
"the world's oldest living and practicing poet. "   The play,
which, as Jacob Adler observes, is considerably more affirmative than much of Williams' earlier work, shows Shannon led back to sanity by Hannah and then delivered to
Maxine, with whom he will presumably live more or less
happily ever after.

On the whole, organized religion comes off rather
badly in this play.   The crew of female Baptists, under the
leadership of Miss Fellowes, are fiendishly hard-hearted
and put fundamental Protestantism in a bad light.   Shannon,
as a failed clergyman of the Episcopal church, makes that
group appear narrow and smug when he describes the difficulties with his congregation (76).

Furthermore, the image of God promoted by these
churches is the same image rejected by J.B. and The Green
Pastures.   Shannon describes this God as "a cruel, senile
delinquent, blaming the world and brutally punishing all he
created for his own faults in construction... " (76).   Because Shannon declines to worship this "angry, petulant old
man, " his congregation has declared him an atheist.

Maxine and Hannah represent two possible alternatives to the religion of the churches. Maxine is a simple
and joyful pagan, a good foil for Shannon's tortured puritanism. Hannah, however, represents the moral and ethical
center of the play. A humanist, her faith has grown out of
her experiences in the world. According to Adler, hers is
a "real and growing belief, requiring neither happiness nor
illusion to nurture it."[19] When Shannon asks her if she believes in God, her reply is "No." She believes instead in
sympathy and compassion between people, in "broken gates
... so they can reach each other..." (95). Unlike Shannon,
who loathes his own weakness and that of others, Hannah
says, "Nothing human disgusts me unless it's unkind, violent" (100).

Hannah shows Shannon that his obsessive guilt is an
exercise in voluptuous self-indulgence. From her he learns
that love and compassion are the way up; and although his
reconciliation has Christian overtones, Hannah, rather than
the church, is the agent of his rebirth. The play, called
"an essay in redemption" by one critic,[20] seems to suggest
that outgrowing formalized religion is one prerequisite to
becoming a mature, loving, even a sane person.

Another play in which institutionalized religion is
strongly criticized is John Guare's The House of Blue
Leaves,[21] winner of both the Circle Award and the Obie in
1970-71. This farce takes place on the day Pope Paul
visited New York. The play uses that occasion to hold the
theatrical and commercial aspects of Roman Catholicism,
that most organized of all religions, up for ridicule.

The main characters in the play, Artie Shaughnessy
and his mistress Bunny, are particularly excited about the
Pope's visit. Bunny, especially, is attracted by the whole

"show biz" aura of the tour, which she compares to the
"premier of Cleopatra." The characters regard the Pope as
in the same class with celebrities like Bob Hope, Jackie
Kennedy, and Johnny Carson. Bunny, for example, wears
an "I Love Paul" button left over from a time when the
Beatles visited New York.

Both Artie and Bunny, who naively expect the Pope
to help them attain the American dream, have personal reasons for wanting to see His Holiness. Artie longs to take
Bunny and run away to Hollywood and achieve instant success as a songwriter. He has, however, formidable com-
plications. For one thing, he writes terrible songs; for
another, his wife, aptly named Bananas, is crazy and he
needs to put her into an institution before he can leave for
the Coast.

Bunny frankly hopes that Bananas will conveniently
die. In fact, she intends to make that her prayer when the
Pope rides by: "It is braided in tall letters, all my veins
and arteries and aortas are braided into the wish that she
dies pretty soon" (25). She also expects the Pope to bless
Artie's music if he will hold sheets of it up when the procession passes by them.

Artie, too, believes in "crawling" to the "Lourdes
and Fatimas" of his future (92). He insists that if Bananas
will kneel down and kiss the television set when the Pope's
image appears on the screen, he will make her well. He
claims to have read an article in The Reader's Digest as-
serting that prayer solves problems. The Digest, he reasons, can't afford to "crap around" (46).

The anti-Catholic satire reaches its height with the
appearance of three celebrity-mad nuns who invade Artie's
house, hoping to see the Pope on television since they

missed seeing him in the street.   The nuns push and shove,
quarrel among themselves, grumble about the quality of the
beer Artie offers them, and complain bitterly because his
television is not a color set.   Like three schoolgirls, they
shriek and squeal when celebrities such as Jackie Kennedy
and Mayor Lindsay appear on the screen.   Finally, when
their boisterous behavior upsets Bananas, Artie asks them
to go into another room, whereupon one of them intones
darkly: "I'm going to start picking who I pray for" (65).

When two of the three are killed in an explosion
created by Ronnie, Artie's demented son (who had intended
the bomb for the Pope), the third says philosophically, "All
they ever wanted to do was die and go to heaven and meet
Jesus." Now, she says, their wish has come true.   The
remaining nun leaves the church when a better offer comes
along.   The convent, she admits, was pretty depressing:
"Pray a while.   Scream a while" (87).   All things considered,
although she had wanted to be the Bride of Christ, she would
rather be a young divorcee (97).

Another aspect of religion subjected to criticism in
prize-winning drama is fanaticism.   Intensity of religious belief, particularly in its more primitive forms, is almost always shown to be unwholesome.   Perhaps the best example
of this attitude can be found in Hatcher Hughes' Pulitzer
Prize winner of 1923-24, Hell-Bent fer Heaven.   This rural
melodrama relies in part upon religion as a means of characterization, for just as the stage Irish are Catholics, hill
folk are usually depicted as ardent practitioners of some
fundamental sect.   This play features a character, Rufe
Pryor, who even in the Bible Belt is considered mildly in-
sane since he got "that camp meetin' brand of religion."
His unctuous quoting of scriptures, his ability to turn any

event into the occasion for a sermonette, his irritating religiosity make some of the other characters doubt the sin-
cerity of his conversion. In fact, one voices the opinion
that he "got religion" to avoid serving in the army.

Rufe is not, however, a simple hypocrite but a dan-
gerous lunatic. He calmly and with malicious intent reacti-
vates an ancient clan feud, then cants about how the Lord
ordained it. Later, hoping to rid himself of a rival for his
sweetheart's hand, he calls upon God to strike the boy down.
Finally, he decides to kill the boy himself (as the Lord's
instrument, of course). When his plans go awry, he renounces his God. Like Abe McCranie, Rufe complains that
God sides with the people who already have all the advantages. The play then restates the idea that although religion
among the lower classes has more immediacy, these have-
nots sometime suspect that their God must favor the haves.

Like Hell-Bent fer Heaven, Lillian Hellman's Toys
in the Attic (Circle Award, 1959-60), presents religious "enthusiasm" as madness. This play, incidentally, reverses
the usual pattern in which primitives or members of the
lower classes are given to intense religious feeling. In this
play, a black man, Henry Simpson, is consistently poised,
articulate, and at all times the voice of reason in the play.
The maniacal young girl, Lily Berniers, is both well born
and well educated. Her religion, however, has not made
her loving or sensitive to the needs of others. In fact,
like Rufe Pryor, Lily is quite capable of cruelty. As one
character puts it, she is still "teething on other people"
(99).

That religion can sometimes be used as a cloak for
cruelty is also strongly suggested in Arthur Miller's The
Crucible, [23] which won him a Tony Award in 1952-53. The

play, set during the time of the Salem witch trials of the
seventeenth century, intends to make a political rather than
a religious statement; but, in spite of the obvious political
parallels to the McCarthy "witch hunts" of the fifties, The
Crucible dramatizes certain religious attitudes.

The action centers around a group of adolescent girls
who claim to have been bewitched. The ensuing panic becomes the occasion for many townspeople to accuse their
neighbors unjustly of commerce with the devil. The accus-
ers are not the victims of mass hysteria but rather of simple
greed. One of the women "cried out" against, for example,
is Elizabeth Proctor, who, upon discovering that Abigail
Williams had seduced her husband John, abruptly dismissed
her from her service. Abigail hopes to win John for herself after Elizabeth is hanged for a witch. Others in Salem
incriminate their neighbors in order to get their land or to
take revenge for past injuries. By the end of the play, the
madness has claimed the lives of many innocent people, including John Proctor himself.

By pointing up its austerity and its hostility to life
The Crucible presents puritanism at its unloveliest. What
this system produces at its worst is exemplified in the person of its official representative, The Rev. Mr. Parris.
Because of Parris' highhanded and undemocratic manner of
running his church, his narrowness, his grasping materialism, and his tendency to preach nothing but hell-fire, his
congregation has split into factions. He views the witch
trials quite cynically as an opportunity to shore up his sag-
ging reputation.

A foil for Parris, however, is the Rev. Mr. Hale of
Beverly, sent to Salem as an expert demonologist. Hale is
a man who, according to Robert Warshow "must have repre-

sented something like the best that Puritan New England had to offer.... "[24]   The course of the trials leads Hale to denounce the proceedings and to warn against adherence to a religion capable of perpetrating such atrocities: "Cleave to no faith," he admonishes, "when faith brings blood" (397).

Two other characters who modify the unflattering view of Puritanism are Rebecca Nurse, a saint by all accounts except those which falsely accused her, and John Proctor. Proctor, it should be noted, is a man who is outgrowing the Puritan view of experience.   He is not a churchgoer, nor a partisan in any of the town's disputes.   One critic, in fact, sees him as something of an eighteenth-century rationalist, a view which needs some qualification in view of Proctor's pervasive sense of guilt about his adultery.

Miller's play deviates from the historical account of the witch trials in that he provides concrete reasons for the "crying out."   One effect he achieves by his de-emphasis of the irrational tendencies of puritanism is to stress its capacity for hypocrisy and brutality.

Many plays, while not actively criticizing religion, imply its bankruptcy as a force in modern life.   Eugene O'Neill's Long Day's Journey into Night[25] (Pulitzer, Circle and Tony awards for 1956-57), a play which one critic calls the "great cultural expression of American Irish Catholicism,"[26] seems to underscore the impossibility of finding strength or solace through religion.   Although Catholicism is a palpable social force among Irish people such as the Tyrones, no one in the Tyrone family can take it seriously or rely on it to alleviate their miseries.   The two Tyrone sons, Jamie and Edmund, are frank non-believers.   Their father, James Tyrone, insists that their apostasy is responsible for their troubles, but the boys think this notion is

"bunk." Mary Tyrone, James' wife, is the most religious
member of the family, but she feels that her drug addiction
has cut her off from the Church. She tries to pray but
says the Blessed Virgin is not going to be fooled by "a lying dope fiend..." (107). She hopes, however, that some-
day she will be forgiven and her faith restored. James admits to being a "bad Catholic in the observance," but he
tells his sons that he believes and that he prays for Mary.
The hopelessness of the play seems to confirm the validity
of Edmund's response when he replies, "Then Nietzsche
must be right. 'God is dead...' " (77-78).

Some of the most powerful plays in the modern
theatre assume that God is indeed dead. Although these
plays do not always provide an answer to the question "What
next?" many do strongly insist on the need to face the truth,
however bleak. Any other stance is shown to be moral cowardice, and the refusal to rid oneself of illusions blocks any
free and creative response to the problem of living in an absurd world.

Edward Albee's controversial play, Who's Afraid of
Virginia Woolf? (Circle and Tony Awards, 1962-63), a
modern secular morality, according to C. W. E. Bigsby,
stresses the destructive and enervating effects of squeamishness in the face of truth. The play revolves around the
emotional orgy of a New England college professor and his
wife on the night in which they "exorcise" their mutual fan-
tasy, an imaginary son. The play ends on an affirmative
note by suggesting that once George and Martha give up
their illusions and accept their own limitations, they will be
saved.

The play, which admits the possibility of salvation,
which shows a son sacrificed for redemption, and which con-

tains an elaborate pattern of religious imagery, actually advances a secular religion as the antidote for escapism and despair. The gospel according to Virginia Woolf, writes Bigsby, is "the primacy of human contact based on an acceptance of reality." Unlike The Cocktail Party which preaches Christianity as the answer to troubled lives, Who's Afraid of Virginia Woolf? suggests liberal humanism as the solution. The play, Bigsby contends, accepts unflinchingly the absurdist vision, but at the same time it transcends despair by allowing the possibility of redemption. "Deprived of God," Bigsby concludes, "man is of necessity his own salvation."[27]

Jack Gelber's Obie winner of 1959-60, The Connection, also presupposes a universe devoid of God, and like Who's Afraid of Virginia Woolf? it suggests, although perhaps more tentatively, the possibility of transcending hopelessness. The Connection presents a group of heroin addicts who for much of the play wait lethargically for the "connection" to arrive with their next fix. This image of the human condition resembles, as many critics have observed, Beckett's vision in Waiting for Godot. Although Kenneth Tynan, in his preface to the play,[28] asks whether the insights provided by heroin might not be as reliable as those supplied by religious mysticism, the play does not show drugs as an acceptable substitute for religion. The addicts in the play "find salvation in junk," according to Robert Brustein,[29] but as Gerald Weales points out, "the salvation is temporary. Only the need is permanent."[30]

Still, in Bigsby's view, The Connection is "a play about the possibility of redemption." Perhaps man can no longer believe in "the big connection," or God; but Solly, the most intelligent of the junkies, does break through to an existentialist understanding which could transcend deterministic absurdity. "You are your own connection, " he says. "It starts and stops here" (26). Although Solly's insight is carried no further, it does, Bigsby notes, inject into the play at least the possibility of freedom. [31]

Taken altogether, the prize-winning plays follow an overall line of development which moves from the position that conventional religion should be humanized to the implication that the Judeo-Christian myth must be discarded altogether in favor of a secular humanism in which man creates and acts out his own salvation. Such plays as Who's Afraid of Virginia Woolf? and The Connection, Night of the Iguana, or The Great White Hope are probably harbingers of a new drama in which the myth that fired the imaginations of centuries of playwrights will be replaced by the religion of man. At any rate, the plays in this group reflect the trend in America as a whole toward secularized religion, a trend which Max Lerner says "turned the main stress of religious energy away from the supernatural to the social, from transcending the human to serving of human needs. "[32] American playwrights, at their best, have used religion in their plays not to justify the ways of God to man, but rather to promote a greater understanding among men.

NOTES

1.   America as a Civilization (New York: Simon and Schuster, 1957), II, 703.

2.   (New York: Harcourt, Brace & Co., 1950).

3.   Carol H. Smith, T. S. Eliot's Dramatic Theory and Practice (Princeton: Princeton Univ. Press, 1963), p. 154.

4. Ibid., p. 163.

5. Denis Donoghue, for example, in The Third Voice (Princeton: Princeton Univ. Press, 1959), says that the real defect of the play is that "the life of the common routine and the way of beatitude" are "totally discrete." Lionel Trilling in The Opposing Self (London: Secker and Warburg, 1955), pp. 145-47, and D. W. Harding in Kenyon Review, XVIII (Summer, 1956) both raise similar objections.

6. Marc Connelly (New York: Twayne Publishers, Inc., 1969), p. 86.

7. Best American Plays, ed. John Gassner (New York: Crown Publishers, Inc., 1963), pp. 589-633.

8. American Plays and Playwrights of the Contemporary Theatre, rev. ed. (New York: Crown Publishers, Inc., 1970), pp. 122-123.

9. Archibald MacLeish (New York: Twayne Publishers, Inc., 1956), p. 139.

10. David Grimstead, Melodrama Unveiled: American Theatre and Culture, 1800-1850 (Chicago: Univ. of Chicago Press, 1968), p. 225.

11. Ibid., pp. 225-226.

12. Best American Plays, ed. John Gassner (New York: Crown Publishers, 1952), pp. 173-203.

13. A New Edition of the Pulitzer Prize Plays, eds. Kathryn Coe and William Cordell (New York: Random House, 1940), pp. 381-426.

14. (New York: New American Library, 1958).

15. (New York: The Dial Press, Inc., 1968).

16. A New Edition of the Pulitzer Prize Plays, pp. 275-316.

17. (New York: The New American Library, 1955).

18. Best American Plays, 1952, pp. 55-104.

19. "Night of the Iguana : A New Tennessee Williams"
     Ramparts, I (Nov., 1962), 59-60.

20. Esther Jackson, The Broken World of Tennessee Wil-
     liams (Madison: The University of Wisconsin Press,
     1965), p. 151.

21. (New York: The Viking Press, 1968).

22. (New York: Random House, 1959).

23. Best American Plays, 1958, pp. 347-402.

24. "The Liberal Conscience in The Crucible, " Arthur
     Miller: A Collection of Critical Essays, ed. Robert
     Corrigan (Englewood Cliffs, N. J.: Prentice-Hall,
     Inc., 1969), p. 113.

25. (New Haven: Yale Univ. Press, 1955).

26. John Henry Raleigh, "O'Neill's Long Day's Journey into
     Night and New England Irish Catholicism, " O'Neill:
     A Collection of Critical Essays, ed. John Gassner
     (Englewood Cliffs, N. J.: Prentice-Hall, 1964), p. 125.

27. Confrontation and Commitment: A Study of Contempo-
     rary American Drama, 1959-1966 (Univ. of Missouri
     Press, 1967), pp. 84-86.

28. (New York: Grove Press, Inc., 1960), p. 9.

29. Seasons of Discontent (New York: Simon and Schuster,
     1959), p. 25.

30. The Jumping-Off Place: American Drama in the 1960's
     (New York: The MacMillan Co., 1969), p. 59.

31. Confrontation and Commitment, pp. 53-54.

32. America as a Civilization, p. 708.

Chapter 6

CONCLUSION

Perhaps, in conclusion, it is useful to confront some of the problems that this study seems to raise and to anticipate questions as to the validity of the method here employed. The selection of five themes as the <u>major</u> ones in American drama, for example, is somewhat arbitrary. Other judges, I am sure, would choose more or fewer and would probably label them differently. Furthermore, it is obviously true that in many cases the themes examined in this study are not the central themes of the plays in which they are examined. Some plays, indeed, are explored again and again for what they suggest about the "major themes," but the central theme of the play is usually not the focal point of the discussion.

A good example of this process is the treatment here of Sidney Howard's comedy, <u>They Knew What They Wanted</u> (Pulitzer, 1924-25). It was analyzed twice in this study, once in Chapter 1 for the assumption it makes about the woman's role, and again in Chapter 2 for what it implies about the relationship between work and material rewards. The play is founded, I have argued, upon two bedrock assumptions: 1) that a woman can find happiness only in marriage, and 2) that in America, a good man, willing to work hard, can get rich. These two ideas are supported both by

the action and by the characterizations; indeed, neither notion is ever seriously questioned.

In spite of the importance of these two assumptions,
however, neither constitutes "the theme" of the play, which
I take to be that mature love--selfless, unpossessive, for-
giving, and grounded in self-knowledge--can overcome all
obstacles.   Howard's purpose was certainly not to provide
a searching exploration of American capitalism or of the so-
ciology of marriage.   In fact, any statement of the central
theme of the play would probably leave aside the very ideas
upon which I have focused, viz., the woman question and the
viability of the American dream.

A play which challenges the assumptions so basic to
Howard's play is Street Scene by Elmer Rice (Pulitzer,
1928-29).   This play concerns New York's huddled masses,
yearning to be free and willing to work but nevertheless unable to collect a share of the American dream.   Street
Scene also vigorously rejects marriage as the solution to a
woman's problems.   In this play, however, as in They Knew
What They Wanted, neither of these two thematic strands is
the main focus of the play.   Rice's chief objective in Street
Scene is to provide a naturalistic slice of New York life so
astonishing in its verisimilitude as to make the audience
say, "This is the way it is."[1]   The two challenges to the
basic assumptions were, then, only tangentially related to
the central purpose, but both were woven deep into the
fabric of the play.

Arthur Miller's play All My Sons (Circle, 1946-47) is
another play I examined for an attitude it expresses rather
than for its primary thematic statement.   The play implies
that the American dream is a tawdry ideal, and it also suggests that war, in spite of its horrors, can be an ennobling

experience. These were the ideas of most significance for my purposes, but Miller's central theme in All My Sons is human brotherhood, which, the play says, transcends the narrow limits of the family. Miller tries to focus the play on the acceptance of Emersonian transcendentalism, with questionable success according to at least one critic. [2] In any case, the two ideas of greatest interest here are both subordinate to the main theme of the play.

Sometimes the idea explored is not only not the main theme, but in fact seems to qualify or contradict the central thematic statement. The central focus of Lorraine Hansberry's A Raisin in the Sun (Circle, 1958-59), for example, is the moral regeneration of Walter Lee Younger, an angry black man on fire with "Charlie fever," the intense need to make money. The events which lead to his eventual awareness that love, family solidarity, and pride in one's heritage are more important than money constitute the main action of the play.

Unconsciously, however, the play seems to affirm an attitude it sets out to deny, for Hansberry makes Walter's salvation contingent upon the receipt of ten thousand dollars. This "specious deus ex machina," as C. W. E. Bigsby observes, seems to "demean the faith in human potential which she is ostensibly endorsing. "[3] Although one could focus upon the artistic weaknesses of the play, its lack of unity, its failure to make a coherent statement, for my purpose-- the examination of basic assumptions, however clumsily expressed--the attitude about the importance of money is extremely significant.

Sometimes, of course, the idea of interest to me happens also to be the central theme of the play. In Why Marry? by Jesse Lynch Williams (Pulitzer, 1917-1918), the mainstream-American assumption that women can find happiness only in marriage, the idea which most interested me, is the theme of the play as well.   I also examined the play for the statements it makes about money and about religion, neither of which is central to the main idea of the play. For the purposes of this study, however, the implication is as useful as the statement; the minor motif as compelling as the central thrust; the unconscious and inartistic exposure of the playwright's bias as interesting as the carefully wrought theme.

Because I did not, as I warned in the introduction, give equal consideration to every prize-winning play, the reader may also legitimately ask whether those plays not discussed in detail or not discussed at all might not qualify the conclusions made here.   Although I should have to concede that such is a possibility, a reading over of the list of winners does not immediately disclose any play which does not either affirm the basic assumptions or challenge them (which is another way of attesting to their viability).

I did not, for example, include a discussion of Tennessee Williams' The Glass Menagerie (Circle, 1944-45), although it comes to mind now as a play which presents a synthesis of the ideas considered in Chapters 1 and 2.   The play, like so many before and after it, demonstrates that although women need economic security (preferably obtained by marriage to a stable and solvent male), men should not settle for a life printed on dollar bills.

The two women in the play, Amanda Wingfield and her daughter Laura, need the protection of a man.   Amanda, to her intense regret, married a charming wanderer who subsequently deserted her and her two children.   That she had other prospects who are now rich and settled makes her present situation especially galling. The daughter's plight, moreover, is worse than the mother's; for while Amanda is determined, shrewd and aggressive, Laura, because she is crippled, is morbidly shy and almost completely introverted. Amanda is managing badly without a husband, but Laura will be doomed without one.

The Glass Menagerie is also in a long line of plays which cast doubts upon the validity of the American dream of success. It suggests that perhaps hard work and a go-getter's determination do not result in one's inevitable mete-oric rise. Jim O'Connor, the gentleman caller Amanda bullies her son Tom into bringing home as a prospective beau for Laura, is a boy with Horatio Alger's dreams, a winning personality, and a willingness to work. In spite of his having been voted "Most Likely to Succeed" by his high school class, Jim has not yet found the way to wealth. Furthermore, the play is slightly contemptuous of the business ethic, as Signi Falk observes, and Williams makes Jim represent the "unimaginative, ambitious, and average young white collar worker."[4] The Glass Menagerie, moreover, calls into question not only the possibility of getting rich in America, but also the efficacy of material success. Although the women need economic security, Tom, with his poet's soul, must break away from the narrow limits of his life--from his dependent family and from his stultifying job in the shoe factory. Thus, The Glass Menagerie brings together two of the staple motifs of prize-winning American drama and accepts two of its most fundamental assumptions.

A recent prize-winner which also exposes the tawdriness of the American dream is Jason Miller's That Championship Season (Circle, 1972).[5] This lacerating play gathers together four of five men who twenty years before had won

a high school basketball championship. The coach, at whose
house they meet for their reunion, prides himself not only
on having forged them into a winning team, but on having
sent them, armed with his success ethic, into the world,
there to continue their winning streak. As the play unfolds,
however, the weaknesses of the men are revealed. George,
the mayor of the town, is exposed as a clumsy and corrupt
politician whose defeat in the coming election seems likely;
James, his campaign manager, is a frustrated junior high
school principal, a man "swallowed up by anonymity"; Tom,
James' brother, the most honest and perceptive of the group,
is an alcoholic. Phil, the only financially successful member of the group, makes a fortune in strip mining, but finds
life so empty that fast women and fast cars are his only
pleasures.

Although the men are all obvious failures, full of
murderous resentment or suicidal self-loathing, the coach
overlooks their character flaws and sprays them constantly
with his Horatio Alger-Vince Lombardi cliches, much as
Willy Loman does his sons. In fact, at one point Tom tells
the coach, as Biff Loman tells Willy, "Stop lying to us.
Stop telling us how great we are" (p. 114).

The coach, a particularly pathetic figure, is exposed
as an unabashed bigot, an ostentatiously pious Catholic with
virulent anti-black, anti-Semitic, pro-McCarthy sentiments.
In spite of his grandiose speeches about how athletics builds
character, the play reveals that his team won the championship because he instructed Martin, the absent member, to
injure one of the players on the opposing team. When Tom
confronts him with this fact, the coach replies that winning
is the only reality.

The play, then, presupposes that the American dream

costs one his humanity and integrity, a pervasive theme in
other prize-winning plays, as I have argued in Chapter 2.
That Championship Season also supports the notion that
American politics is corruptive, one of the themes explored
in Chapter 4. To George and his cohorts, patronage, character assassination and illegal contributions are the politician's stock in trade. Finally, the play contains that thread
of skepticism so familiar in American prize-winning plays
about the efficacy of institutionalized religion, a point discussed in Chapter 5. Thus the play, a resounding success
both on and off Broadway, is also rock-ribbed, mainstream
American drama in its fundamental assertions about American life.

Another question the reader of this study might legitimately raise concerns the plays which did not receive consideration here because they did not win one of the prizes I
somewhat arbitrarily chose to consider. Might they not perhaps make different assumptions about American life? It is
possible. I do not (of course) speak with authority about
those other plays. A brief examination of the serious con-
tenders in one season of the 1920's and another of the
1930's was instructive, however, for the non-prize winners
seemed to support the same value structure as do the prize-
winning plays.

During the season of 1926-27, the year the Pulitzer
jurors made their highly controversial selection of Paul
Green's play, In Abraham's Bosom, the other important
plays were The Road to Rome by Robert E. Sherwood, Saturday's Children by Maxwell Anderson, and The Silver Cord
by Sidney Howard.

Sherwood's The Road to Rome[6] falls into the minority
category of plays with a pacifist theme. A frothy comedy

with serious philosophical undercurrents, the play has
Amytis, the half-Greek wife of the Roman dictator Fabius
Maximus, seduce Hannibal on the night before he plans to
sack Rome.   The antithesis of austere Roman virtue (and
dullness), Amytis convinces Hannibal of the absurdity of
war: "Every sacrifice made in the name of war," she argues, "is wasted."   The meeting between the two provides
Sherwood an opportunity to express his anti-war sentiments;
in fact, according to Baird Shuman, the play is "diluted with
speeches about the futility of war" and marred by "pacifist
monologues."[7]

When Hannibal, converted by Amytis' argument and
further swayed by her considerable charms, turns away
from the gates of Rome, the play suggests that his act is a
victory for humanity, decency, and plain common sense.
Although Eleanor Flexner has complained that Hannibal's retreat signified his emasculation, "the man of force and action" made "the victim of abstract ideas,"[8] Sherwood could
hardly have calculated such a response, for he clearly intended the play to make an anti-war statement.   He later
wrote, in fact, that he had inserted a message into the play:
"That message," he said, "was that I was opposed to war."[9]
Like many American playwrights, Sherwood had an ambivalent attitude about war and violence; he would in his later
plays, espouse the necessity of fighting for a just cause.
The Road to Rome, however, is perfectly consistent with
the pacifist sentiments in many plays after World War I, including one of Sherwood's prize-winners, Idiot's Delight.

Maxwell Anderson's comedy, Saturday's Children,[10]
another contender in 1926-27, is generally consistent with
the assumptions discussed in Chapter 1, namely, that marriage is the spoiler of hopes and dreams.   As I have argued

above, most American prize-winning plays insist that a woman must marry, but they do not often picture marriage as
conducive to happiness.

Saturday's Children features Bobby Halevy, unmarried
at twenty-three and beginning to be anxious about it. Her
alternatives are to "be an old maid and a public charge, " or
to find a husband. When a likely prospect, Rims O'Neil,
appears, Bobby, coached by her married sister Florrie,
captures him in the time-honored way. Her marriage proves
an immediate disappointment when she becomes Rims' servant rather than his sweetheart. Burdened with domestic
chores and with more bills than Rims' salary can cover,
and resentful because Rims comes and goes as he pleases
while she is pinned down at home, Bobby grows restive.
Sister Florrie counsels that having a baby is the classic way
to tie a man down for good, but Bobby, tired of tricks,
leaves Rims and moves into a boardinghouse. Rims, now
wild with jealousy because Bobby has her job back and receives gentlemen callers, visits her room at night as a
clandestine lover rather than a husband.

The play is basically anti-marriage. Florrie's marriage is presumably typical of most, a point she keeps emphasizing when the naive Bobby objects to deception. Marriage, one gathers from Florrie's experience, begins in
trickery and is followed by a series of power struggles (eu-
phemistically called "the period of adjustment") which deter-
mine which partner's freedom will be most curtailed. Once
that is settled, the couple begins the long, dull descent into
settled middle-age.

The strongest voice raised against conventional marriage is Mr. Halevy's. He confesses that he never wanted
his daughter to marry. Girls, he says, are brought up "all

for the service and delight" of their husbands. Men at least
can have a good time--fall in love, have an affair and, when
it ends, get out. When Bobby asks why one could not have
a love affair and then get married, he replies: "Marriage
is no love affair. It's ... last year's love affair. It's a
house and bills and dishpans and family quarrels. That's
the way the system beats you" (p. 390).

Like so many prize-winning plays, Saturday's Children poses the problem without providing a solution. Living
in a rented room under the eye of a tyrannical landlady and
having one's lovers crawl through the window is hardly a
serious, permanent solution to the disagreeable aspects of
marriage. Like Why Marry? and Street Scene, the play
dramatizes the difficulties, but its failure to suggest a reasonable alternative is significant. In Saturday's Children,
as in most prize-winning plays as well, there is none.

Sidney Howard's The Silver Cord[11] also treats the
woman's role and starts from the usual assumptions. This
play, like Howard's prize-winner, Craig's Wife, shows the
unmasking of a horrifying woman. It also depicts the grim-
ness of family life, showing it up as a seed-bed, a forcing
house of neurotic behavior. Like Nina Leeds in Strange
Interlude (Pulitzer, 1927-28), Mrs. Phelps has no life that
is not lived through someone else. Like Nina, she is a
parasitic growth, but while Nina has two husbands and a
lover as well as a son, Mrs. Phelps has, except for five
years of an unhappy marriage, devoted herself exclusively
to her two sons.

Her relationship with the two boys, of course, is extremely unwholesome. Coy and flirtatious, she primps and
poses before them, calling them "her two beaux." She also
dishes out guilt, reminding them of her weak heart and of

her enormous sacrifices on their behalf.   Motivated by sexual jealousy, she tries during most of the play to break up
the romance of her younger son Robert and the marriage of
her older son David.   David's wife, Christine, sees through
Mrs. Phelp's machinations at once, and as soon as she has
guaged the depth of the problem, forces David to choose between her and his mother.   David, by choosing Chris, is
saved; Robert, however, is "engulfed forever."

In the character of Christine, the play, like Jesse
Lynch Williams' Why Marry?, presents the "new woman."
A foil for her mother-in-law, Christine, a Heidelburg-
trained doctor, is career-oriented, competent, independent.
Also like Why Marry?, the play does not suggest that the
single life for such a woman is desirable.   In fact, one
flaw in the play is its failure to explain why such a woman
as Chris would want to marry David Phelps and conceive a
child in the first weeks of marriage.

The play expresses the familiar pro-marriage bias in
several ways.   One is the implication that remarriage would
have prevented Mrs. Phelps' fanatical devotion to her sons.
Even her unhappy marriage to her first husband would have
been better than widowhood, both for her and for her two
boys.   Furthermore, the play never suggests that the best
thing for Christine would be the collapse of her marriage to
David.   The question the play poses is the same one put by
a column in a well-known women's magazine: "Can This
Marriage Be Saved?"   At no time in the play is the question ever, "Should This Marriage be Saved?"   In The Silver
Cord, as in most popular American drama, even a strong,
intelligent woman needs a husband, regardless of how weak
or disagreeable he may prove to be.

The theatre season of 1934-35 yielded a rich harvest

of plays, the worst of which was probably the Pulitzer Prize
winner, Zoe Akins' The Old Maid, a sentimental melodrama,
but one which conformed in all particulars to the popular
mythology concerning women, marriage, and motherhood.
Passed over were two plays now considered classics in
American dramatic literature, Clifford Odets' Awake and
Sing and Lillian Hellman's The Children's Hour. Although
both of these plays are artistically superior to the Pulitzer
prize-winner, both are solidly grounded in the traditional
American assumptions about life as they are expressed in
prize-winning plays.

The case of Clifford Odets is a puzzling one. Although he was widely considered the successor of Eugene
O'Neill, his plays never received any major drama award.
Odets had, of course, leftist leanings; one is, therefore,
tempted to assume that the obvious Marxist fervor in his
plays precluded their winning prizes in an essentially bourgeois theatre. Such a hypothesis is dubious when one considers that many other American playwrights--Elmer Rice
and Arthur Miller, to mention only two--have been considered left of center and have nevertheless been heaped
with honors. More to the point, perhaps, is that Odets'
plays, particularly Awake and Sing, [12] are solidly in the
American grain. The values in Awake and Sing are the
same ones insisted upon in play after play since the establishment of drama prizes in this country.

Set in the Bronx during the Depression, the play,
like The Glass Menagerie, depicts a disintegrating family.
Everyone in the Berger family has problems, but the play
focuses upon Ralph, a young man torn between his desire to
marry his sweetheart and live a conventional life and his
need to make a total commitment to social justice and hu-

man betterment. His uncle Jacob serves both as the voice
of his conscience and as a choral figure who, as Gerald
Rabkin observes, provides explicit social commentary by
"drawing a Marxist moral from the statements and activi-
ties of other characters."[13]

In the end, Ralph chooses social commitment rather
than pursuit of selfish and personal dreams. He will work,
as Uncle Jacob had urged him to do, for a world where
"life won't be printed on dollar bills." With its assertion
that a life printed on dollar bills is no life at all, Awake
and Sing can be classified with dozens of antimaterialistic
prize-winning plays, for this idea is one of four or five
virtually unchallenged in popular American drama.

The play also assumes, moreover, all the usual
things about the roles of men and women. Bessie Berger,
Ralph's mother, is a courageous woman trying to hold her
family together, but like so many women in these plays,
she has a thirst for security and thus is materialistic.
Furthermore, she is a bully and a scold. She runs the
family, wears the pants, and although it seems clear that
her husband Myron has abdicated his position as head of the
household, Bessie has assumed the role with disastrous results. The play implies that the traditional roles are best
and that a system which permits or encourages a woman to
get out of her place is bad. Indeed, according to one critic
of Odets' plays, Bessie's dominant position in the family
"underlies the play's theme that modern society, with its
overemphasis on money, perverts natural family relationships."[14]

Interestingly enough, although the play assumes the
conventional marriage values for women, it also shows marriage as a lower order of business than that of the serious

work of the world. Like Men in White, the play says that
if a man wants to make a serious contribution to the race,
he will put marriage out of his mind or far down on his list
of priorities.

Like Clifford Odets, Lillian Hellman has never won
the Pulitzer Prize, although she has received the Circle
Award twice. It was not her political sentiments that kept
her from winning the Pulitzer, but rather the squeamishness
of judges confronted with a play about lesbianism. "Unmen-
tioned censorship," wrote one theatre historian, made The
Children's Hour ineligible in "the silliest and most disgrace-
ful decision in the 50-year history of the Prize...."[15]

The play concerns two schoolteachers whose lives are
ruined when a vicious pupil accuses them of being lovers.
Although the subject of lesbianism was a sensational one in
the 1930's, the play in no way challenges the usual American
assumption about the proper relationship between men and
women. In fact, The Children's Hour reinforces the notion
that the single woman's life is a life of horrors and dramatizes the idea that a woman's salvation lies only in marriage.
Because they are single women, Karen and Martha are sus-
ceptible to suspicion and gossip. The play contains not a
hint, not the merest suggestion, that homosexual relationships are an alternative to heterosexual ones. The under-
current of sexual attraction that Martha has for Karen leads
to jealousy, heartache, disgrace and, in Martha's case,
death. Karen, too, faces a bleak future, for the incident
has cost her the marriage that would have saved her. Thus,
although the subject of The Children's Hour was offensive to
some, the play itself is completely affirmative if not down-
right moralistic about conventional marriage values.

One wing of the American theatre which is popularly

supposed to be the most defiant and the most contemptuous of the traditional American values is Off-Off Broadway. It strikes me that most of the defiance and contempt in the Off-Off Broadway theatre, however, expresses itself in the use of shocking language, of nudity, of explicit sex, and unconventional theatrical techniques. Aside from these obvious departures from bourgeois theatre, many of the plays themselves are saying the same things that American plays have always said.

For the critic away from New York, the plays of Off-Off are often inaccessible. Some find their way to uptown theatres and thereby enter the larger cultural stream, some are published and made available to readers outside the New York area; but many spring up like mushrooms, flourish for a few days, a week or two at most, then disappear. Of those plays which do filter out, my general impression is that they are not radically different in their assumptions from older and more popular American plays.

A play which illustrates my argument well is The Great American Desert[16] by Joel Oppenheimer, the first play produced by the Judson Poets' Theatre, in November of 1961. As its name suggests, the play concerns the West, but the treatment of the subject is unconventional. Bearing many of the hallmarks of the Off-Off Broadway product, The Great American Desert is multileveled and freely mixes poetry, philosophy, and put-on with a naturalistic story of three cowboys. Oppenheimer's purpose appears to be the demythicization of the West enshrined in the imaginations of audiences brought up on Hollywood and television versions.

The three cowboys in this play, on the run after robbing a bank, are not the priggish and impossibly stoic, laconic, fearless, and chaste cowboys of the mythic treatment.

They whine about the food and the heat, quarrel about the
distribution of chores, confess to worries about their sexual
prowess and fret about the possibility of Indian attacks.
One of them, a gunfighter, has a venereal disease and is a
drug addict. All three are profane. They are, in short,
recognizable human beings rather than stereotypical Western
heroes.

The play further debunks the heroic stereotype by
having four legendary heroes--Wyatt Earp, Wild Bill Hickok,
Doc Holliday, and Billy the Kid--speak as if from heaven,
revealing that their exploits may have been the result of
psychological disturbances of one sort or another.

In spite of the grimly naturalistic approach, the
characters in the play are treated with sympathy, even with
admiration. Oppenheimer wrote recently in a letter about
his play, "What I was saying basically was that life in 1870
on the great plains was not much different from life in 1960
in the big city...." The Great American Desert may be an
irreverent and unflattering comment on the myth, but it is a
warm, almost tender comment upon the men. The play ex-
hibits a kind of respect for the heroes of the West that the
critics of violent America seldom have. Caught up in the
vast movements of history and trying to survive day by day,
the men of the West were violent and sometimes they en-
joyed it. They were for the most part, however, just "doin'
their part, " whatever that happened to be. In its rather
casual acceptance of the necessity of violence, Oppenheimer's play is not far removed from the majority of prize-
winning plays which treat the same subject.

What this study has revealed, finally, it seems to
me, is that no American play is that far removed in its basic assumptions from any other American play. They have

always said the same few things: that people need freedom
in order to flourish; that rampant capitalism is finally unworkable; that the worship of Mammon is self-defeating; that
politics encourages corruption; that organized religions can
be the last refuge of hypocrites; that jingoism and chauvinism
are stupid; and that war and violence are terrible, but sometimes necessary and even ennobling. Until such time as
these cease to be the fundamental beliefs of most people in
America, one can anticipate that American plays will continue to reflect them.

NOTES

1. Frank Durham, Elmer Rice (New York: Twayne Publishers, Inc., 1970), p. 60.

2. C. W. E. Bigsby, Confrontation and Commitment
   (Columbia, Mo.: University of Missouri Press, 1968),
   p. 31.

3. Ibid., p. 159.

4. Tennessee Williams (New York: Twayne Publishers,
   Inc., 1961), p. 77.

5. (New York: Atheneum, 1972).

6. Twenty-Five Best Plays of the Modern American
   Theatre, ed. John Gassner (New York: Crown Publishers, Inc., 1949).

7. Robert E. Sherwood (New York: Twayne Publishers,
   Inc., 1964), p. 38.

8. American Playwrights, 1918-1938 (New York: Simon
   and Schuster, 1938), p. 274.

9. There Shall Be No Night (New York: Charles Scribner's Sons, 1940), pp. xii-xiii.

10. Twenty-Five Best Plays of the Modern American

Theatre, ed. John Gassner (New York: Crown Publishers, Inc., 1949).

11. (New York: Charles Scribner's Sons, 1927).

12. Masters of Modern Drama, ed. Haskell Block and
Robert G. Shedd (New York: Random House, 1962).

13. Drama of Commitment (Bloomington, Ind.: Indiana
University Press, 1964), p. 184.

14. Edward Murray, Clifford Odets: The Thirties and After
(New York: Frederic Ungar Publishing Co., 1968),
p. 34.

15. John Toohey, A History of the Pulitzer Prize Plays
(New York: Citadel Press, 1967), p. 128.

16. The Off Off Broadway Book: The Plays, People,
Theatre, ed. Albert Poland and Bruce Mailman (New
York: Bobbs-Merrill Co., Inc., 1972).

BIBLIOGRAPHY

A. PRIMARY SOURCES

Plays

Abbot, George, and Jerome Weidman. Fiorello! New York: Random House, 1960.

Akins, Zoe. The Old Maid. New York: Appleton-Century Co., 1934.

Albee, Edward. A Delicate Balance. New York: Atheneum, 1966.

_____. Who's Afraid of Virginia Woolf? in Best American Plays, 1957-1963, ed. John Gassner. New York: Crown Publishers, Inc., 1963.

Anderson, Maxwell. Both Your Houses. New York: Samuel French, 1933.

_____. Saturday's Children, in Twenty-Five Best Plays of the Modern American Theatre, ed. John Gassner. New York: Crown Publishers, Inc., 1949.

_____. Winterset. Washington, D.C.: Anderson House, 1935.

Connelly, Marc. The Green Pastures, in A New Edition of the Pulitzer Prize Plays, ed. Kathryn Coe and William Cordell. New York: Random House, 1940.

Davis, Owen. Icebound, in A New Edition of the Pulitzer Prize Plays, ed. Kathryn Coe and William Cordell. New York: Random House, 1940.

de Hartog, Jan. The Fourposter, in Best American Plays,

1951-1957, ed. John Gassner. New York: Crown
Publishers, Inc., 1958.

Eliot, Thomas Stearns. The Cocktail Party. New York:
Harcourt, Brace and Co., 1950.

Frings, Ketti. Look Homeward, Angel, in Best American
Plays, 1958-1963, ed. John Gassner. New York:
Crown Publishers, Inc., 1963.

Gale, Zona. Miss Lulu Bett, in A New Edition of the Pulitzer Prize Plays, ed. Kathryn Coe and William Cordell. New York: Random House, 1940.

Gelber, Jack. The Connection. New York: Grove Press,
Inc., 1960.

Gibson, William. Dinny and the Witches and The Miracle
Worker: Two Plays. New York: Atheneum, 1960.

Gilroy, Frank. The Subject Was Roses. New York: Random House, 1965.

_____. Who'll Save the Plowboy? New York: Random
House, 1962.

Glaspell, Susan. Alison's House, in A New Edition of the
Pulitzer Prize Plays, ed. Kathryn Coe and William
Cordell. New York: Random House, 1940.

Goodrich, Frances, and Albert Hackett. The Diary of Anne
Frank. New York: Random House, 1956.

Gordone, Charles. No Place to be Somebody. New York:
Bobbs-Merrill Co., Inc., 1969.

Green, Paul. In Abraham's Bosom, in A New Edition of the
Pulitzer Prize Plays, ed. Kathryn Coe and William
Cordell. New York: Random House, 1940.

Guare, John. The House of Blue Leaves. New York: The
Viking Press, 1968.

Hansberry, Lorraine. A Raisin in the Sun. New York:
New American Library, 1958.

Heggen, Thomas, and Joshua Logan. Mister Roberts, in

Best American Plays, 1945-1951, ed. John Gassner. New York: Crown Publishers, Inc., 1952.

Hellman, Lillian. The Children's Hour, in Twenty Best Plays of the Modern American Theatre, ed. John Gassner. New York: Crown Publishers, Inc., 1939.

_____. Toys in the Attic. New York: Random House, 1960.

_____. Watch on the Rhine, in Four Plays by Lillian Hellman. New York: Random House, 1942.

Howard, Sidney. The Silver Cord. New York: Charles Scribner's Sons, 1927.

_____. They Knew What They Wanted, in A New Edition of the Pulitzer Prize Plays, ed. Kathryn Coe and William Cordell. New York: Random House, 1940.

Hughes, Hatcher. Hell-Bent fer Heaven, in A New Edition of the Pulitzer Prize Plays, ed. Kathryn Coe and William Cordell. New York: Random House, 1940.

Inge, William. Picnic. New York: Random House, 1953.

Jones, LeRoi. Dutchman and The Slave. New York: William Morrow and Co., 1964.

Kaufman, George, and Morrie Ryskind. Of Thee I Sing, in A New Edition of the Pulitzer Prize Plays, ed. Kathryn Coe and William Cordell. New York: Random House, 1940.

_____, and Moss Hart. You Can't Take It With You, in A New Edition of the Pulitzer Prize Plays, ed. Kathryn Coe and William Cordell. New York: Random House, 1940.

Kelly, George. Craig's Wife, in A New Edition of the Pulitzer Prize Plays, ed. Kathryn Coe and William Cordell. New York: Random House, 1940.

Kingsley, Sidney. Darkness at Noon, in Best American Plays, 1945-1951, ed. John Gassner. New York: Crown Publishers, Inc., 1952.

_____. Men in White, in A New Edition of the Pulitzer
Prize Plays, ed. Kathryn Coe and William Cordell.
New York: Random House, 1940.

_____. The Patriots, in The Critics' Prize Plays.
Cleveland: The Word Publishing Co., 1945.

Kramm, Joseph. The Shrike. New York: Random House,
1952.

Lindsay, Howard, and Russel Crouse. State of the Union,
in Best American Plays, 1945-1951, ed. John Gassner. New York: Crown Publishers, Inc., 1952.

Lowell, Robert. The Old Glory. Farrar, Straus, and
Giroux, 1964.

McCullers, Carson. The Member of the Wedding, in Best
American Plays, 1945-1951, ed. John Gassner. New
York: Crown Publishers, Inc., 1952.

MacLeish, Archibald, J.B., in Best American Plays, 1957-
1963, ed. John Gassner. New York: Crown Publishers, Inc., 1963.

Miller, Arthur. All My Sons. New York: Reynal and
Hitchcock, 1947.

_____. The Crucible, in Best American Plays, 1951-
1957, ed. John Gassner. New York: Crown Publishers, Inc., 1958.

_____. Death of a Salesman, in Masters of Modern
Drama, ed. Haskell Block and Robert Shedd. New
York: Random House, 1962.

Miller, Jason. That Championship Season. New York:
Atheneum, 1972.

Mosel, Tad. All the Way Home, in Best American Plays,
1957-63, ed. John Gassner. New York: Crown
Publishers, Inc., 1963.

Nolan, Paul T. The Loneliest Game. Houston: The Edgemoor Press, 1973.

Odets, Clifford. Awake and Sing, in Masters of Modern

Drama, ed. Haskell Block and Robert G. Shedd. New
York: Random House, 1962.

O'Neill, Eugene. Anna Christie, in A New Edition of the
Pulitzer Prize Plays, ed. Kathryn Coe and William
Cordell. New York: Random House, 1940.

_____. Beyond the Horizon, in A New Edition of the
Pulitzer Prize Plays, ed. Kathryn Coe and William
Cordell. New York: Random House, 1940.

_____. Long Day's Journey Into Night. New Haven:
Yale University Press, 1955.

_____. Strange Interlude, in A New Edition of the Pul-
itzer Prize Plays, ed. Kathryn Coe and William Cordell. New York: Random House, 1940.

Oppenheimer, Joel. The Great American Desert, in The
Off Off Broadway Book: The Plays, People, Theatre,
ed. Albert Poland and Bruce Mailman. New York:
Bobbs-Merrill Co., Inc., 1972.

Rabe, David. The Basic Training of Pavlo Hummel and
Sticks and Bones: Two Plays by David Rabe. New
York: Viking Press, 1973.

Rice, Elmer. Street Scene, in A New Edition of the Pulitzer Prize Plays, ed. Kathryn Coe and William Cordell. New York: Random House, 1940.

Sackler, Howard. The Great White Hope. New York: The
Dial Press, 1968.

Saroyan, William. The Time of Your Life, in Famous
American Plays of the 1930's. New York: Dell Publishing Co., 1959.

Schary, Dore. Sunrise at Campobello. New York: Random House, 1957.

Sherwood, Robert E. Abe Lincoln in Illinois, in A New Edition of the Pulitzer Prize Plays, ed. Kathryn Coe and
William Cordell. New York: Random House, 1940.

_____. Idiot's Delight, in A New Edition of the Pulitzer
Prize Plays, ed. Kathryn Coe and William Cordell.

New York: Random House, 1940.

_____. The Road to Rome, in Twenty-Five Best
Plays of the Modern American Theatre, ed.
John Gassner. New York: Crown Publishers, Inc.,
1949.

_____. There Shall Be No Night. New York: Charles
Scribner's Sons, 1940.

Steinbeck, John. Of Mice and Men, in The Critics' Prize
Plays. Cleveland: The World Publishing Co., 1945.

Van Druten, John. I Am A Camera, in Best American
Plays, 1951-1957, ed. John Gassner. New York:
Crown Publishers, Inc., 1958.

Wilder, Thornton. The Skin of Our Teeth. New York:
Harper and Bros., 1942.

_____. Our Town, in A New Edition of the Pulitzer
Prize Plays, ed. Kathryn Coe and William Cordell.
New York: Random House, 1940.

Williams, Jesse Lynch. Why Marry? New York: Charles
Scribner's Sons, 1914.

Williams, Tennessee. Cat on a Hot Tin Roof. New York:
New American Library, 1955.

_____. The Glass Menagerie, in Masters of Modern
Drama, ed. Haskell Block and Robert Shedd. New
York: Random House, 1962.

_____. Night of the Iguana, in Best American Plays,
1945-1951, ed. John Gassner. New York: Crown
Publishers, Inc., 1952.

_____. The Rose Tattoo, in Best American Plays, 1951-
57, ed. John Gassner. New York: Crown Publishers,
Inc., 1958.

_____. Streetcar Named Desire, in Best American Plays,
1945-1951, ed. John Gassner. New York: Crown
Publishers, Inc., 1952.

B. SECONDARY SOURCES

1. Books

Adams, James Truslow. The Epic of America. Boston:
    Little, Brown and Company, 1931.

Allen, Frederick Lewis. Only Yesterday. New York: The
    Perennial Library, 1964.

Bigsby, C. W. E. Confrontation and Commitment: A Study
    of Contemporary American Drama. Columbia, Mo.:
    Univ. of Missouri Press, 1967.

Brown, H. Rap. Die Nigger Die! New York: The Dial
    Press, 1969.

Brown, John Mason. Dramatis Personae. New York: Vik-
    ing Press, 1963.

_____. Two on the Aisle. New York: W. W. Norton,
    1938.

Brustein, Robert. Seasons of Discontent. New York: Si-
    mon and Schuster, 1959.

Carpenter, Frederic I. American Literature and the Dream.
    New York: Philosophical Library, Inc., 1955.

_____. Eugene O'Neill. New York: Twayne Publishers,
    Inc., 1964.

Cawelti, John. Apostles of the Self-Made Man: Changing
    Concepts of Success in America. Chicago: The Uni-
    versity of Chicago Press, 1965.

Clurman, Harold. The Naked Image. New York: The
    Macmillan Company, 1966.

Donoghue, Denis. The Third Voice. Princeton: Princeton
    University Press, 1959.

Durham, Frank. Elmer Rice. New York: Twayne Pub-
    lishers, Inc., 1970.

Dusenbury, Winifred. The Theme of Loneliness in Modern

American Drama.   Gainesville, Fla.:   University of
Florida Press, 1960.

Falk, Doris.   Eugene O'Neill and the Tragic Tension.   New
Brunswick, N.J.:   Rutgers University Press, 1958.

Falk, Signi.   Archibald MacLeish.   New York: Twayne Publishers, Inc., 1965.

Flexner, Eleanor.   American Playwrights, 1918-1938.   New
York: Simon and Schuster, 1938.

Floan, Howard.   William Saroyan.   New York: Twayne Publishers, Inc., 1966.

Freedman, Morris.   American Drama in Social Context.
Carbondale: Southern Illinois Press, 1971.

Friedan, Betty.   The Feminine Mystique.   New York: W.
W. Norton, 1963.

Gagey, Edmond M.   Revolution in American Drama.   New
York: Columbia University Press, 1947.

Gassner, John.   Dramatic Soundings.   New York: Crown
Publishers, Inc., 1968.

Greer, Germaine.   The Female Eunuch.   New York: Bantam Books, 1970.

Grimstead, David.   Melodrama Unveiled: American Theatre
and Culture, 1800-1850.   Chicago: University of
Chicago Press, 1968.

Huber, Richard.   The American Idea of Success.   New
York: McGraw-Hill Book Company, 1971.

Jackson, Esther Merle.   The Broken World of Tennessee
Williams.   Madison: The University of Wisconsin
Press, 1965.

Lash, Joseph P.   Eleanor and Franklin.   New York: W. W.
Norton and Company, 1971.

Lerner, Max.   America as a Civilization.   2 vols.   New
York: Simon and Schuster, 1957.

Lesy, Michael. Wisconsin Death Trip. New York: Pantheon, 1973.

Levy, Valerie B. Violence as Drama: A Study of the Development of the Use of Violence on the American Stage. Diss., Claremont College, 1970.

Lewis, Allan. American Plays and Playwrights of the Contemporary Theatre. New York: Crown Publishers, Inc., 1970.

Lynn, Kenneth. The Dream of Success: A Study of the Modern American Imagination. Boston: Little, Brown and Company, 1955.

Moses, Montrose J. Dramas of Modernism and Their Forerunners. New York: Little, Brown and Company, 1931.

Murray, Edward. Clifford Odets: The Thirties and After. New York: Frederic Ungar Publishing Co., 1968.

Nannes, Caspar. Politics in the American Drama. Washington, D. C.: The Catholic University Press, 1960.

Nolan, Paul T. Marc Connelly. New York: Twayne Publishers, Inc., 1969.

Quinn, Arthur Hobson, ed. Contemporary American Plays. New York: Scribner's, 1923.

_____. A History of American Drama from the Civil War to the Present Day. New York: Harper and Bros., 1927.

Rabkin, Gerald. Drama of Commitment: Politics in the American Theatre of the Thirties. Bloomington: The Indiana University Press, 1964.

Shuman, Baird. Robert E. Sherwood. New York: Twayne Publishers, Inc., 1964.

Slotkin, Richard. Regeneration Through Violence: The Mythology of the American Frontier, 1600-1860. Middleton, Conn.: The Wesleyan University Press, 1973.

Smith, Carol H. T. S. Eliot's Dramatic Theory and Prac-
    tice. Princeton: Princeton University Press, 1963.

Smith, Grover. T. S. Eliot's Poetry and Plays. Chicago:
    The University of Chicago Press, 1956.

Stuckey, W. J. The Pulitzer Prize Novels: A Critical Back-
    ward Look. Norman: The University of Oklahoma
    Press, 1966.

Tolstoy, Leo. Anna Karenina, tr. Constance Garnett.
    Garden City: Doubleday and Company, 1946.

Toohey, John. A History of the Pulitzer Prize Plays. New
    York: Citadel Press, Inc., 1967.

Trilling, Lionel. The Opposing Self. London: Secker and
    Warburg, 1955.

Violence and the Struggle for Existence, ed. David N.
    Daniels, Marshall F. Gilula, and Frank M. Ochburg.
    Boston: Little, Brown and Company, 1970.

Weales, Gerald. The Jumping-Off Place: American Drama
    in the 1960's. New York: The Macmillan Company,
    1969.

Wertham, Frederic. A Sign for Cain: An Exploration of
    Human Violence. New York: Warner Books, Inc.,
    1969.

Wyllie, Irvin G. The Self-Made Man in America: The Myth
    of Rags to Riches. New Brunswick, N. J.: Rutgers
    University Press, 1954.

2. Articles

Adler, Jacob. "Night of the Iguana : A New Tennessee
    Williams?" Ramparts, I (November, 1962), 59-68.

_____. "Shakespeare in Winterset, " Educational Theatre
    Journal, VI (1954), 241-248.

Carpenter, Frederic I. "Focus on Eugene O'Neill's The
    Iceman Cometh, " in American Dreams, American Night-
    mares, ed. David Madden. Carbondale: Southern

Illinois Press, 1970, pp. 158-164.

Eisinger, Charles E. "Focus on Arthur Miller's Death of a
    Salesman: The Wrong Dreams, " in American Dreams,
    American Nightmares, ed. David Madden. Carbon-
    dale: Southern Illinois University Press, 1970,
    pp. 165-174.

Foster, Richard J. "Confusion and Tragedy: The Failure
    of Miller's Salesman, " in Two Modern American
    Tragedies: Reviews and Criticism, ed. John Hurrell.
    New York: Charles Scribner's Sons, 1961, pp. 82-88.

Hagopian, John V. "Arthur Miller: The Salesman's Two
    Cases, " Modern Drama, VI (Oct., 1963), 117-125.

Harding, D. W. "Progression of Theme in Eliot's Modern
    Plays, " Kenyon Review, XVIII (Summer 1956), 337-
    360.

Hodgson, Godfrey. "Do Schools Make a Difference?" At-
    lantic Monthly (March, 1973), pp. 33-46.

Jones, LeRoi. "Brief Reflections on Two Hot Shots, " Kul-
    ture, III (Winter, 1963), 3-5.

Jones, Robert Emmet. "Tennessee Williams' Early Hero-
    ines, " Modern Drama, II (December, 1959), 211-219.

Kaplan, Charles. "Two Depression Plays and Broadway's
    Popular Idealism, " American Quarterly, XV (1963),
    579-585.

Lampson, Harold. "Review: Who's Afraid of Virginia
    Woolf?" Saturday Review (June 29, 1963).

Nolan, Paul T. "God on Stage: A Problem in Characteri-
    zation in Marc Connelly's The Green Pastures, "
    Xavier University Studies, IV (May, 1965), 75-84.

_____. "Marc Connelly's 'Divine Comedy': Green Pas-
    tures Revisited, " Western Speech, XXX (Fall, 1966),
    216-224.

THE PRIZE-WINNING PLAYS

1917-18: Pulitzer   Jesse Lynch Williams' Why Marry?

            Passed Up   The Copperhead, A Tailor Made Man, Seventeen, and The Country Cousin

1918-19: Pulitzer   No Award

            Passed Up   Lightnin', Three Wise Fools, A Little Journey, and East is West

1919-20: Pulitzer   Eugene O'Neill's Beyond the Horizon

            Passed Up   The Famous Mrs. Fair, Adam and Eve, Clarence, and Declasse

1920-21: Pulitzer   Zona Gale's Miss Lulu Bett

            Passed Up   The First Year, The Emperor Jones, The Bad Man and Nice People

1921-22: Pulitzer   Eugene O'Neill's Anna Christie

            Passed Up   Dulcy, Six Cylinder Love, To the Ladies, The Hero, and The Hairy Ape

1922-23: Pulitzer   Owen Davis' Icebound

            Passed Up   The Adding Machine, You and I, The Torchbearers, The Fool, and Why Not?

1923-24: Pulitzer   Hatcher Hughes' Hell-Bent fer Heaven

            Passed Up   The Changelings, Tarnish, and Sun-Up

1924-25:   Pulitzer   Sidney Howard's They Knew What
                         They Wanted

           Passed Up   What Price Glory?, Desire Under the
                         Elms, Processional, Minick, The
                         Youngest, and Dancing Mothers

1925-26:   Pulitzer   George Kelly's Craig's Wife

           Passed Up   The Wisdom Tooth, The Butter and
                         Egg Man, The Great God Brown, and
                         Lucky Sam McCarver

1926-27:   Pulitzer   Paul Green's In Abraham's Bosom

           Passed Up   The Silver Cord, Broadway, Satur-
                         day's Children, and The Road to
                         Rome

1927-28:   Pulitzer   Eugene O'Neill's Strange Interlude

           Passed Up   Coquette, The Royal Family, Porgy,
                         Paris Bound and Behold the Bride-
                         groom

1928-29:   Pulitzer   Elmer Rice's Street Scene

           Passed Up   Holiday, The Front Page, Gypsy,
                         Machinal, and Gods of the Lightening

1929-30:   Pulitzer   Marc Connelly's The Green Pastures

           Passed Up   The Criminal Code, The Last Mile,
                         June Moon, Rebound, and Hotel Uni-
                         verse

1930-31:   Pulitzer   Susan Glaspell's Alison's House

           Passed Up   Elizabeth the Queen, Once in a Life-
                         time, Tomorrow and Tomorrow,
                         Green Grow the Lilacs, and Five-
                         Star Final

1931-32:   Pulitzer   George Kaufman and Morrie Rys-
                         kind's Of Thee I Sing

           Passed Up   Mourning Becomes Electra, The

House of Connelly, Reunion in Vienna,
Counsellor-at-Law, and The Animal
Kingdom

1932-33:   Pulitzer   Maxwell Anderson's Both Your Houses

           Passed Up   One Sunday Afternoon; Dinner at
                         Eight; We, the People; Alien Corn,
                         and Biography

1933-34:   Pulitzer   Sidney Kingsley's Men in White

           Passed Up   Mary of Scotland, Ah, Wilderness,
                         Dodsworth, Yellow Jack, They Shall
                         Not Die, and Tobacco Road

1934-35:   Pulitzer   Zoe Akins' The Old Maid

           Passed Up   The Children's Hour, Awake and Sing,
                         The Petrified Forest, Valley Forge,
                         Rain from Heaven, and Merrily We
                         Roll Along

1935-36:   Pulitzer   Robert E. Sherwood's Idiot's Delight

           Circle   Maxwell Anderson's Winterset

           Passed Up   First Lady, Paradise Lost, Dead
                         End, Ethan Frome, and Porgy and
                         Bess

1936-37:   Pulitzer   George Kaufman and Moss Hart's
                         You Can't Take It With You

           Circle   Maxwell Anderson's High Tor

           Passed Up   Johnny Johnson, Excursion, The Wo-
                         men, and Having Wonderful Time

1937-38:   Pulitzer   Thornton Wilder's Our Town

           Circle   John Steinbeck's Of Mice and Men

           Passed Up   Golden Boy, Susan and God, On Bor-
                         rowed Time, and Prologue to Glory

1938-39:   Pulitzer   Robert E. Sherwood's Abe Lincoln

		in Illinois
	Circle	No Award
	Passed Up	The Little Foxes, My Heart's in the Highlands, Rocket to the Moon, The Philadelphia Story, and No Time for Comedy
1939-40:	Pulitzer	William Saroyan's The Time of Your Life
	Circle	William Saroyan's The Time of Your Life
	Passed Up	Life with Father, The Male Animal, The Man Who Came to Dinner, and Mornings at Seven
1940-41:	Pulitzer	Robert E. Sherwood's There Shall Be No Night
	Circle	Lillian Hellman's Watch on the Rhine
	Passed Up	Native Son, Lady in the Dark, and Claudia
1941-42:	Pulitzer	No Award Given
	Circle	No Award Given
	Passed Up	In Time to Come, The Moon Is Down, Junior Miss, Candle in the Wind, and The Land Is Bright
1942-43:	Pulitzer	Thornton Wilder's The Skin of Our Teeth
	Circle	Sidney Kingsley's The Patriots
	Passed Up	The Eve of St. Mark and Tomorrow the World
1943-44:	Pulitzer	No Award
	Circle	No Award

	Passed Up	Winged Victory, The Searching Wind, and Oklahoma
1944-45:	Pulitzer	Mary Chase's Harvey
	Circle	Tennessee Williams' The Glass Menagerie
	Passed Up	A Bell for Adano, The Late George Apley, Anna Lucasta, I Remember Mama, and Soldier's Wife
1945-46:	Pulitzer	Howard Lindsay and Russel Crouse's State of The Union
	Circle	No Award
	Passed Up	Home of the Brave, The Magnificent Yankee, Deep Are the Roots, Born Yesterday, and Dream Girl
1946-47:	Pulitzer	No Award
	Circle	Arthur Miller's All My Sons
	Passed Up	The Iceman Cometh, and Another Part of the Forest
1947-48:	Pulitzer	Tennessee Williams' A Streetcar Named Desire
	Circle	Tennessee Williams' A Streetcar Named Desire
	Tony	Thomas Heggen and Joshua Logan's Mister Roberts
	Passed Up	Command Decision, The Heiress, and Allegro
1948-49:	Pulitzer	Arthur Miller's Death of a Salesman
	Circle	Arthur Miller's Death of a Salesman
	Tony	Arthur Miller's Death of a Salesman
	Passed Up	Anne of a Thousand Days, Detective

Story, Life With Mother, and The
Silver Whistle

1949-50:	Pulitzer	Oscar Hammerstein and Joshua Logan's South Pacific
	Circle	Carson McCullers' The Member of the Wedding
	Tony	T. S. Eliot's The Cocktail Party
	Passed Up	Come Back, Little Sheba
1950-51:	Pulitzer	No Award
	Circle	Sidney Kingsley's Darkness at Noon
	Tony	Tennessee Williams' The Rose Tattoo
	Passed Up	The Autumn Garden and The Country Girl
1951-52:	Pulitzer	Joseph Kramm's The Shrike
	Circle	John Van Druten's I Am a Camera
	Tony	Jan de Hartog's The Fourposter
	Passed Up	Point of No Return, Mrs. McThing, and Jane
1952-53:	Pulitzer	William Inge's Picnic
	Circle	William Inge's Picnic
	Tony	Arthur Miller's The Crucible
	Passed Up	Camino Real, On Borrowed Time, The Climate of Eden and The Time of the Cuckoo
1953-54:	Pulitzer	John Patrick's The Teahouse of the August Moon
	Circle	John Patrick's The Teahouse of the August Moon

Tony	John Patrick's The Teahouse of the August Moon
Passed Up	Tea and Sympathy, The Caine Mutiny Court Martial, and Take a Giant Step
1954-55:	Pulitzer	Tennessee Williams' Cat on a Hot Tin Roof
	Circle	Tennessee Williams' Cat on a Hot Tin Roof
	Tony	Joseph Hayes's The Desperate Hours
	Passed Up	The Flowering Peach, The Bad Seed, Bus Stop, and Inherit the Wind
1955-56:	Pulitzer	Frances Goodrich and Albert Hackett's The Diary of Anne Frank
	Circle	Frances Goodrich and Albert Hackett's The Diary of Anne Frank
	Tony	Frances Goodrich and Albert Hackett's The Diary of Anne Frank
	Obie	No American Award
	Passed Up	A View from the Bridge, No Time for Sergeants, A Hatfull of Rain, Middle of the Night
1956-57:	Pulitzer	Eugene O'Neill's Long Day's Journey Into Night
	Circle	Eugene O'Neill's Long Day's Journey Into Night
	Tony	Eugene O'Neill's Long Day's Journey Into Night
	Passed Up	Orpheus Descending, A Moon for the Misbegotten, A Clearing in the Woods, and Auntie Mame
1957-58:	Pulitzer	Ketti Frings' Look Homeward, Angel

Circle	Ketti Frings' Look Homeward, Angel
Tony	Dore Schary's Sunrise at Campobello
Obie	No American Award
Passed Up	The Dark at the Top of the Stairs, Two for the Seesaw, West Side Story, The Rope Dancers, and The Music Man
1958-59: Pulitzer	Archibald MacLeish's J.B.
Circle	Lorraine Hansberry's A Raisin in the Sun
Tony	Archibald MacLeish's J.B.
Obie	No American Award
Passed Up	A Touch of the Poet, Sweet Bird of Youth, The Disenchanted and The Pleasure of His Company
1959-60: Pulitzer	George Abbot and Jerome Weidman's Fiorello!
Circle	Lillian Hellman's Toys in the Attic
Tony	William Gibson's The Miracle Worker
Obie	Jack Gelber's The Connection
Passed Up	The Tenth Man, The Andersonville Trial, A Loss of Roses, and The Best Man
1960-61: Pulitzer	Tad Mosel's All the Way Home
Circle	Tad Mosel's All the Way Home
Tony	No American Award
Obie	No American Award
Passed Up	Mary, Mary; A Far Country; Big Fish, Little Fish; The Wall; and

Advise and Consent

1961-62:	Pulitzer	Abe Burrows, Jack Weinstock, and Willie Gilbert's How to Succeed in Business Without Really Trying
	Circle	Tennessee Williams' Night of the Iguana
	Tony	No American Award
	Obie	Frank Gilroy's Who'll Save the Plowboy?
	Players'	Gerald Sanford's Children of the Center Ring
	Passed Up	Gideon; Oh Dad, Poor Dad, Mama's Hung You in the Closet and I'm Feeling So Sad; A Thousand Clowns and Purlie Victorious
1962-63:	Pulitzer	No Award
	Circle	Edward Albee's Who's Afraid of Virginia Woolf?
	Tony	Edward Albee's Who's Afraid of Virginia Woolf?
	Obie	No Award
	Players'	Vincent Longhi's Climb the Greased Pole
	Passed Up	The Milk Train Doesn't Stop Here Any More; Natural Affection; Never Too Late; My Mother, My Father, and Me
1963-64:	Pulitzer	No Award
	Circle	No American Award
	Tony	No American Award
	Obie	LeRoi Jones' Dutchman

	Players'	Paul T. Nolan's There's Death for the Lonely
	Passed Up	After the Fall, The Passion of Joseph D., Barefoot in the Park, The Ballad of the Sad Cafe, and Any Wednesday
1964-65:	Pulitzer	Frank Gilroy's The Subject Was Roses
	Circle	Frank Gilroy's The Subject Was Roses
	Tony	Frank Gilroy's The Subject Was Roses
	Obie	Robert Lowell's The Old Glory
	Players'	Richard Stockton's One World at a Time
	Passed Up	Luv, The Odd Couple, Slow Dance on the Killing Ground, Incident at Vichy, and Tiny Alice
1965-66:	Pulitzer	No Award
	Circle	No American Award
	Tony	No American Award
	Obie	Ronald Ribman's Journey of the Fifth Horse
	Passed Up	Generation, Hogan's Goat, Cactus Flower, and The Lion in Winter
1966-67:	Pulitzer	Edward Albee's A Delicate Balance
	Circle	No American Award
	Tony	No American Award
	Obie	No Award
	Passed Up	America, Hurrah; You Know I Can't Hear You When the Water's Running;

The Star-Spangled Girl; MacBird!;
The Deer Park; and Don't Drink the
Water

1967-68: Pulitzer   No Award

          Circle   No Award

          Tony   No Award

          Obie   No American Award

          Passed Up   Scuba Duba, The Price, Plaza Suite,
                        I Never Sang for My Father, The
                        Boys in the Band

1968-69: Pulitzer   Howard Sackler's The Great White
                        Hope

          Circle   Howard Sackler's The Great White
                        Hope

          Tony   Howard Sackler's The Great White
                        Hope

          Obie   No Award

          Passed Up   Forty Carats, Ceremonies in Dark
                        Old Men, We Bombed in New Haven,
                        In the Bar of a Tokyo Hotel, and
                        Adaptation/Next, 1776

1969-70: Pulitzer   Charles Gordone's No Place to Be
                        Somebody

          Circle   Paul Zindel's The Effects of Gamma
                        Rays on Man-in-the Moon Marigolds

          Tony   No American Award

          Obie   Tie: Paul Zindel's The Effects of
                        Gamma Rays on Man-in-the-Moon
                        Marigolds and Megan Terry's Ap-
                        proaching Simone

          Passed Up   Indians, Butterflies Are Free, The
                        Last of the Red Hot Lovers, and

Child's Play

1970-71:   Pulitzer   Paul Zindel's The Effects of Gamma
                          Rays on Man-in-the-Moon Marigolds

           Circle   John Guare's The House of Blue
                          Leaves

           Tony   No American Award

           Obie   John Guare's The House of Blue
                          Leaves

           Passed Up   Steambath, The Trial of the Catons-
                          ville Nine, The Gingerbread Lady,
                          All Over, and And Miss Reardon
                          Drinks a Little

1971-72:   Pulitzer   No Award

           Circle   Jason Miller's That Championship
                          Season

           Tony   David Rabe's Sticks and Bones

           Obie   The Mutation Show

           Passed Up   Where Has Tommy Flowers Gone?,
                          Small Craft Warnings, Ain't Supposed
                          to Die a Natural Death, The Prison-
                          er of Second Avenue

1972-73:   Pulitzer   Jason Miller's That Championship
                          Season

           Circle   No American Award

           Tony   Jason Miller's That Championship
                          Season

           Obie   Tie: Joseph A. Walker's The River
                          Niger and Sanford Wilson's The Hot
                          L Baltimore

           Passed Up   The Creation of the World and Other
                          Business, The Sunshine Boys, and
                          A Little Night Music

Index